The Divine Masculine:

A Journey for the Queer Male

Pete Cossaboon

ISBN: **9798302777010**

DEDICATION

To the countless opportunities for growth and empowerment that have come my way, disguised as challenges and obstacles, I extend my deepest gratitude. It is through these experiences that I have come to understand my own innate divinity and the power that lies within each of us.

I envision a world where every individual recognizes their own divine nature, stepping into their personal power and manifesting a life filled with purpose, love, and abundance. May this book serve as a catalyst for that transformation, inspiring each reader to embrace their true self and create a life beyond their wildest dreams.

Together, let us embark on this journey of self-discovery, empowerment, and spiritual growth, co-creating a world that is a reflection of our highest potential and deepest desires.

Love. Peace. Release.

Table of Contents

Part 4: Pathways to Empowerment

11. **The Spiritual Warrior: Overcoming Shadows**
- Techniques to face and transcend personal and societal shadows.
12. **The Alchemical Process of Transformation**
- Turning pain into power through rituals and mindfulness.
13. **The Role of Ritual in Queer Masculinity**
- Designing and embracing personal rites of passage.
14. **Embodied Masculinity: Physical Practices for Empowerment**
- Yoga, meditation, and somatic experiences to anchor empowerment.

Part 5: The Queer Male as Healer and Visionary

15. **The Queer Prophet: Redefining Leadership**
- Gay men as catalysts for cultural and spiritual evolution.
16. **Sacred Sexuality: Healing Through Pleasure**
- Honoring the sacredness of queer intimacy and relationships.
17. **Creative Masculinity: Art, Play, and Self-Expression**
- How creativity becomes a transformative masculine power.
18. **Queer Brotherhood: Building Authentic Connections**
- Fostering community and support within the LGBTQ+ space.

Part 6: Embodying the Divine Masculine

19. **The Divine Masculine in Action**
- Daily practices to live as an integrated and empowered individual.
20. **Epilogue: The Future of Masculine Consciousness**
- Envisioning a world healed and uplifted through the queer divine masculine.

Foreword: A Note from the Author

The journey of a gay man through life is one of constant interplay, a dance between energies that both define us and challenge us. In the broader human story, archetypes such as the nurturer, protector, destroyer, organizer, and creator weave together to form a complex tapestry of masculine and feminine dynamics. For us, these archetypes resonate differently. They manifest in ways that defy traditional norms, offering both liberation and profound complexity.

Unlike conventional masculine ideals, which often define success through rigid roles and expectations, we have no universally accepted standards for who we are supposed to be. Traditional societal guidelines—family structures, relationship norms, modes of dress—do not necessarily fit us, nor do they leave room for our unique perspectives. As a result, we are left to forge our own paths, discovering not only who we are but also how we can exist authentically in a world that is often not designed for us.

This duality is both a gift and a challenge. On one hand, it allows us the freedom to express ourselves in ways that transcend the heteronormative box, embracing the full spectrum of our identity and creative power. On the other hand, it demands an acute awareness of our environment and our place within it. To live outside the mainstream narrative is to navigate a world where authenticity must coexist with survival, and where self-expression must find a balance with external expectations.

Living in this space, we are called to develop a heightened level of consciousness. We must be attuned to our own needs, desires, and dreams while remaining vigilant to the realities of a world that can sometimes be harsh and unyielding. This balancing act requires a strength that is uniquely ours—a strength rooted in resilience, adaptability, and the ability to hold the tension of opposites.

As gay men, we often inhabit dual roles: visionaries who imagine a better world, and pragmatists who understand the rules of the current one. We are creators of new paradigms, but also protectors of our safety and well-being. We are nurturers of our inner truth, yet we must navigate external structures that do not always honor it. This reality shapes us into beings of profound depth, capable of immense growth, creativity, and transformation.

This book is an exploration of these dynamics—a guide to understanding the interplay of masculine and feminine energies within us and how they can be harnessed to live a more empowered, fulfilling life. It is a call to embrace our unique path with courage and clarity, to celebrate our individuality while acknowledging the challenges we face. In doing so, we claim our rightful place as integral contributors to the broader human story.

May this work serve as a beacon, illuminating the ways we can live authentically, thrive creatively, and stand proudly in our truth, even in the face of adversity. It is a journey worth undertaking, and I am honored to walk it with you.

Part 1: Foundations of the Divine Masculine

Introduction: Rediscovering the Divine Masculine

The concept of the divine masculine is as old as humanity itself, woven into the myths, spiritual traditions, and cultural practices of civilizations across the globe. It is a force that transcends gender and sexuality, representing archetypal energies such as strength, leadership, protection, and creation. In its highest form, the divine masculine exists not as a rigid standard but as a fluid and evolving energy—a balance of power and vulnerability, structure and freedom, logic and intuition. Yet, for queer men, this concept carries additional layers of complexity, challenge, and profound opportunity.

Historically, the divine masculine has often been presented through heteronormative lenses, emphasizing traditional roles such as the father, the warrior, and the patriarch. These depictions, while valuable in some contexts, often exclude or marginalize queer experiences. For gay men, these archetypes can feel alien or even oppressive, as they fail to account for the nuanced ways in which we express masculinity. This exclusion has left many of us questioning our place in the grand narrative of what it means to embody masculine energy.

However, history reveals a different story when we dig deeper. In many indigenous and ancient cultures, queer individuals were seen not as outsiders but as integral members of the community. From the two-spirit traditions of Native American tribes to the shamanic roles held by queer individuals in cultures spanning Asia, Africa, and the Pacific Islands, there is a rich heritage of queer men serving as spiritual leaders, healers, and visionaries. In these roles, they bridged the gap between masculine and feminine, embodying the duality and wholeness that the divine masculine seeks to express.

In modern times, the divine masculine remains profoundly relevant for queer men. While society has evolved in many ways, traditional masculine ideals still dominate much of the cultural narrative. Strength is often equated with aggression, leadership with dominance, and emotional vulnerability with weakness. For queer men, navigating these expectations can feel like a constant balancing act—striving to honor our own truths while existing in a world that does not always value them.

This unique position offers both challenges and opportunities. The absence of rigid societal roles for queer men frees us to explore masculinity in ways that are authentic and expansive. We are not confined by the expectations of the heteronormative world, which allows us to redefine strength, love, and power on our terms. Yet, this freedom comes with the responsibility of forging new pathways and creating models of masculinity that resonate with our experiences.

Rediscovering the divine masculine means moving beyond outdated notions of what it means to be a man. It involves embracing the full spectrum of archetypal energies—protector and nurturer, creator and destroyer, leader and supporter. For queer men, it also means recognizing and honoring the feminine energies that flow alongside the masculine within us, forming a harmonious interplay that is uniquely ours.

In this exploration, the divine masculine becomes a source of empowerment, healing, and transformation. It allows us to claim our strength without denying our sensitivity, to lead without controlling, and to create without destroying. It invites us to step into our full power as individuals and as a collective, contributing to a world that celebrates diversity in all its forms.

As we embark on this journey, we will explore the cultural, historical, and spiritual roots of the divine masculine, as well as its modern relevance for queer men. Through archetypal wisdom, practical tools, and deep reflection, we will uncover the ways in which this ancient force can guide us toward greater authenticity, fulfillment, and connection. The divine masculine is not a relic of the past; it is a living, breathing energy that holds the key to our present and future. Let us rediscover it together.

Historical Perspectives: Gay Men as Spiritual Leaders

Throughout history, gay men have played vital roles as spiritual leaders, visionaries, and mediators between the human and divine. In cultures across the world, individuals who embodied both masculine and feminine traits were often revered, their unique perspectives seen as a bridge between opposing forces. These individuals were entrusted with sacred responsibilities, guiding their communities through spiritual, emotional, and even practical challenges. By exploring indigenous cultures, mythology, and spirituality, we can uncover a rich legacy that challenges modern notions of masculinity and celebrates the profound contributions of queer men.

The Two-Spirit Tradition

Among Indigenous cultures in North America, the concept of "Two-Spirit" individuals offers a powerful example of how gender and sexuality were historically understood in ways that transcended rigid binaries. Two-Spirit individuals were recognized as embodying both masculine and feminine energies, making them uniquely equipped to fulfill roles that required balance, insight, and a deep connection to the spiritual world.

The term "Two-Spirit," while modern in origin, reflects traditional Indigenous beliefs that predate colonization. Each tribe had its own terminology, rituals, and roles for these individuals, but common themes included their roles as healers, shamans, teachers, and ceremonial leaders. For example, the Lakota referred to such individuals as *winkte*, and the Zuni people honored the *lhamana*. Far from being marginalized, Two-Spirit people were often revered and seen as essential to the health and harmony of their communities.

Two-Spirit individuals were frequently tasked with roles that bridged the physical and spiritual realms. They acted as intermediaries during rituals, healers who utilized their intuitive understanding of both masculine and feminine energy, and keepers of sacred knowledge. Their ability to "see beyond" the ordinary world allowed them to provide unique insights, whether through dreams, visions, or spiritual practices.

In many tribes, the recognition of a child as Two-Spirit was a cause for celebration. This identity was seen as a divine gift, a calling to live a life of service and connection to higher realms. They were often granted freedoms and responsibilities that others were not, serving as both caretakers of their communities and conduits for the sacred.

Global Mythologies and Spiritual Traditions

The reverence for queer individuals is not limited to Indigenous cultures. Around the world, myths and spiritual traditions have celebrated figures who embodied a blend of masculine and feminine energies, recognizing them as embodiments of divine balance and wisdom.

- **Hindu Traditions**: The figure of *Ardhanarishvara*, a composite of the god Shiva and the goddess Shakti, represents the unity of masculine consciousness and feminine energy. This androgynous deity exemplifies the sacred balance necessary for creation and highlights the spiritual potential of integrating both forces within oneself.
- **Classical Greece**: Figures like the god Dionysus were associated with fluidity in gender and sexuality. Dionysus, the god of wine, ecstasy, and transformation, blurred the lines between masculine and feminine, offering a powerful example of how non-conformity can be a source of divine inspiration and liberation.
- **Polynesian Cultures**: In Polynesian societies, the *mahu* of Hawaii and the *fa'afafine* of Samoa were recognized as a third gender. These individuals often served as cultural stewards, caretakers, and spiritual leaders, embodying a balance that enriched their communities.
- **Ancient American Civilizations**: In the Mayan and Aztec civilizations, gender-variant individuals were

integral to religious ceremonies. They were often considered sacred and believed to have special access to divine wisdom.

The Sacred Roles of Queer Men

Across these diverse traditions, a common thread emerges: queer men were often seen as spiritually attuned beings who could transcend the limitations of binary thinking. By embodying both masculine and feminine qualities, they provided their communities with insights that others could not. Their fluidity was not a liability but a strength, allowing them to adapt, mediate, and innovate in ways that enriched their societies.

In these roles, queer men were not constrained by traditional family structures or rigid gender expectations. This freedom enabled them to devote their lives to spiritual growth, communal care, and creative expression. By stepping outside conventional roles, they became agents of transformation, guiding others toward greater understanding and connection.

Lessons for Today

The historical reverence for queer individuals as spiritual leaders offers a powerful counterpoint to the marginalization often experienced in modern societies. It reminds us that our unique identities are not barriers to spiritual connection but gateways to profound wisdom and strength.

For gay men today, reclaiming this legacy can be an act of empowerment and healing. By understanding our historical roles as nurturers, healers, and visionaries, we can reframe our identities as sources of strength and inspiration. The divine masculine, in this context, becomes not a rigid standard but an expansive energy that allows us to embody our full potential.

As we rediscover this rich heritage, we honor not only those who came before us but also the possibilities that lie within ourselves. In embracing our roles as spiritual leaders, we continue a tradition of transformation, creativity, and balance that has the power to shape our communities and the world.

The Crisis of Masculine Identity

Masculinity is in crisis. This statement resonates not only with those exploring the concept of manhood in modern society but also with those who have experienced its challenges firsthand. For queer men, this crisis is particularly acute. The journey toward understanding and embodying authentic masculinity is often complicated by societal expectations, internal conflicts, and the shadow of patriarchal structures. At the heart of this crisis lies a fundamental misunderstanding of what masculinity truly is and how it can be expressed in its highest, most authentic form.

Shadow Masculinity vs. the Divine Masculine

The shadow masculine represents a distorted, incomplete, and often destructive form of masculinity. It arises when the true essence of the divine masculine is suppressed, misunderstood, or warped by societal pressures. The shadow masculine manifests in traits such as aggression, domination, emotional repression, and a relentless pursuit of power at the expense of others. It is driven by fear—fear of vulnerability, fear of failure, and fear of losing control.

In contrast, the divine masculine represents a balanced, mature, and life-affirming expression of masculinity. It is characterized by qualities such as strength tempered with compassion, leadership rooted in service, and power guided by wisdom. The divine masculine does not seek to dominate but to uplift, to create, and to protect. It is an energy that nurtures both self and others, embracing vulnerability as a source of strength.

For queer men, the challenge lies in navigating a world where the shadow masculine is often celebrated while the divine masculine is undervalued or ignored. The dominant culture frequently equates masculinity with dominance, emotional stoicism, and heteronormative family structures, leaving little room for alternative expressions of manhood. Queer men, who often embody a blend of masculine and feminine energies, find themselves at odds with these limited definitions.

How Patriarchy Distorts Authentic Masculinity for Queer Men

Patriarchy, the system that has long governed societal structures, is one of the primary forces behind the crisis of masculine identity. It imposes rigid expectations on men, defining success through control, competition, and conformity. Under patriarchy, masculinity is reduced to a narrow set of traits, leaving little space for individuality, emotional depth, or authentic self-expression.

For queer men, the impact of patriarchy is doubly harmful. Not only are they excluded from traditional notions of manhood, but they are also subjected to stigmatization and marginalization. Patriarchy views deviation from its prescribed norms as a threat, often responding with hostility or erasure. As a result, queer men are forced to navigate a landscape where their identities are invalidated, and their expressions of masculinity are dismissed or ridiculed.

This distortion creates a profound internal conflict for many queer men. On one hand, they may feel pressured to conform to societal standards of masculinity to gain acceptance or avoid discrimination. On the other hand, they may yearn to express their true selves, embracing the fluidity and complexity that define their unique experiences. This tension can lead to feelings of inadequacy, shame, and alienation, as they struggle to reconcile their inner truth with external expectations.

The Way Forward: Embracing the Divine Masculine

The path to resolving the crisis of masculine identity lies in rediscovering and embracing the divine masculine. This involves moving beyond the limitations of patriarchal norms and shadow masculinity to cultivate a more expansive and authentic understanding of what it means to be a man.

For queer men, this journey begins with self-acceptance and self-awareness. By acknowledging and honoring their unique blend of masculine and feminine energies, they can redefine masculinity on their own terms. This process requires letting go of societal judgments and internalized shame, recognizing that their identity is not a weakness but a strength.

The divine masculine invites queer men to embody qualities such as courage, integrity, and empathy while remaining true to their individuality. It challenges them to lead with their hearts as well as their minds, to create from a place of love rather than fear, and to build connections that uplift rather than divide.

In this reimagining of masculinity, queer men can find a sense of purpose and empowerment that transcends societal limitations. They become not only participants in but also leaders of a new narrative—one that celebrates diversity, authenticity, and the transformative power of love.

As we confront the crisis of masculine identity, it is essential to recognize that this is not merely a personal struggle but a collective one. By reclaiming the divine masculine, queer men have the potential to heal not only themselves but also the broader cultural wounds inflicted by patriarchy and shadow masculinity. This transformation begins with a simple yet profound truth: masculinity, in its highest form, is a force for good, and every man has the capacity to embody it in his own unique way.

Part 2: Archetypes of the Divine Masculine

The King: Leadership and Purpose

The King archetype is the cornerstone of the divine masculine, representing leadership, purpose, and a deep sense of responsibility. It embodies the qualities of self-sovereignty, balance, and alignment with a higher purpose. For queer men, stepping into the King archetype is not about conforming to patriarchal notions of power but about reclaiming a form of leadership that is authentic, inclusive, and empowering.

The Essence of the King Archetype

At its core, the King archetype is about self-sovereignty—the ability to govern one's own life with clarity, integrity, and purpose. A true King does not impose authority through dominance but inspires loyalty and respect through wisdom and fairness. The King understands that leadership begins within, rooted in self-awareness and a commitment to aligning actions with values.

The King archetype encompasses both power and responsibility. Power, in this context, is not about control over others but the ability to influence and guide with intention and compassion. Responsibility is the willingness to be accountable for one's actions and to serve as a steward of both personal growth and communal well-being.

For queer men, the King archetype invites us to redefine what it means to lead. It challenges us to reject the toxic models of masculinity often promoted by society and instead cultivate a style of leadership that reflects our unique strengths and experiences. As Kings, we create spaces where authenticity is celebrated, diversity is honored, and collective growth is prioritized.

Self-Sovereignty: Ruling Your Inner Kingdom

Self-sovereignty begins with the recognition that each of us is the ruler of our inner kingdom. This kingdom consists of our thoughts, emotions, desires, and actions. A sovereign King does not allow external circumstances or other people's expectations to dictate his life. Instead, he cultivates self-mastery, ensuring that his inner world remains balanced and aligned.

To achieve self-sovereignty, we must first confront the aspects of ourselves that are out of alignment. These may include fears, doubts, or unresolved wounds that undermine our ability to lead. By addressing these challenges with honesty and courage, we reclaim our inner power and establish a foundation of strength and stability.

Practices that support self-sovereignty include:

- **Reflection and Self-Inquiry**: Regularly examining your beliefs, values, and goals to ensure they reflect your true self.
- **Boundaries**: Setting clear limits to protect your energy and maintain alignment with your purpose.
- **Mindfulness**: Developing the ability to respond to life's challenges with clarity and presence rather than reacting from a place of fear or insecurity.

Inner Alignment: The Key to Authentic Leadership

True leadership arises from inner alignment—a state where thoughts, emotions, and actions are in harmony. When we are aligned, we radiate a sense of purpose and confidence that inspires others to trust and follow us. Alignment also allows us to make decisions that are both intuitive and logical, balancing our masculine and feminine energies.

For queer men, inner alignment often requires navigating and integrating diverse aspects of identity. The King archetype provides a framework for this integration, helping us to honor all parts of ourselves while maintaining a clear sense of direction. By embracing our unique perspectives and experiences, we become leaders who can bridge divides and build connections.

The Shadow King

Like all archetypes, the King has a shadow side. When distorted, the King becomes either a tyrant or a weakling.

- **The Tyrant King**: Driven by insecurity and fear, this shadow seeks to control others through manipulation, aggression, or intimidation. The Tyrant King demands loyalty without earning it, using power to serve his ego rather than the greater good.
- **The Weakling King**: This shadow abdicates responsibility, avoiding challenges and refusing to take decisive action. The Weakling King is often consumed by self-doubt, unable to trust himself or others.

Both shadows arise when we lose touch with the divine masculine's essence. To embody the King fully, we must recognize and transform these shadow aspects, returning to a place of balance and authenticity.

Creating Your Inner Kingdom

To step into the King archetype, we must first envision the kind of kingdom we wish to create. This kingdom represents not only our inner world but also the impact we hope to have on those around us. What values will your kingdom uphold? What legacy will you leave behind?

Practical steps to create your inner kingdom include:

1. **Define Your Vision**: Clarify your purpose and the values that guide your life.
2. **Embody Your Power**: Cultivate confidence and assertiveness while remaining grounded in empathy and fairness.
3. **Lead by Example**: Align your actions with your principles, inspiring others through your integrity.
4. **Serve Others**: Use your strengths to uplift and support those in your community, creating a ripple effect of positive change.

The King's Role in the Collective

The King archetype is not solely about personal growth; it is also about serving the collective. A true King understands that his power is a gift to be used for the greater good. He creates a kingdom where all are empowered to thrive, recognizing that his strength is measured not by how much he takes but by how much he gives.

For queer men, the King archetype offers a path to leadership that is inclusive, transformative, and deeply aligned with our values. By embodying the King, we reclaim our power, rewrite the narrative of masculinity, and create a world where authenticity reigns.

The King is within you, waiting to be awakened. Will you answer his call?

The Warrior: Courage and Action

The Warrior archetype is the embodiment of courage, action, and discipline. It is the force within us that rises to meet challenges, protects what is sacred, and pursues goals with unwavering focus. For queer men, the Warrior takes on a unique role: it is not only a defender of the self but also an advocate for authenticity in a world that often demands conformity. Embracing the Warrior archetype requires developing personal discipline, setting clear boundaries, and standing strong in the face of adversity.

The Essence of the Warrior

The Warrior is not merely about physical strength or aggression; it is about purposeful action guided by clarity and integrity. A true Warrior fights not for domination or ego but to uphold truth, justice, and the values that define their core. This archetype thrives on discipline and commitment, ensuring that efforts are directed toward meaningful goals rather than wasted on distractions.

For queer men, the Warrior often manifests as a protector of authenticity. Living outside the heteronormative framework frequently requires courage—courage to express oneself fully, to defy societal expectations, and to advocate for one's place in the world. The Warrior's energy empowers us to face these challenges with resilience and determination.

Courage in the Face of Adversity

Courage is the hallmark of the Warrior. It is the ability to act despite fear, uncertainty, or opposition. For queer men, this courage often involves confronting internal and external battles:

- **Internal Courage**: Overcoming self-doubt, internalized shame, or limiting beliefs.
- **External Courage**: Navigating a world that may not always accept or understand our identity.

The Warrior archetype invites us to see fear not as a barrier but as an opportunity for growth. By acknowledging our fears and acting in alignment with our values, we transform them into stepping stones toward empowerment.

Mastering Personal Discipline

Discipline is the foundation of the Warrior's strength. It is the ability to stay focused on a goal, persevere through challenges, and maintain integrity in the face of temptation or distraction. For queer men, discipline often means staying true to our authentic selves while navigating a world that may encourage us to conform or compromise.

Practical ways to cultivate personal discipline include:

1. **Set Clear Goals**: Identify what matters most to you and create a plan to achieve it.
2. **Build Consistent Habits**: Small, regular actions build the resilience and focus needed for larger battles.
3. **Develop Emotional Discipline**: Learn to respond to challenges with clarity rather than reacting impulsively.
4. **Celebrate Progress**: Acknowledge your victories, no matter how small, to stay motivated and aligned.

Discipline is not about perfection; it is about persistence. The Warrior knows that setbacks are inevitable but sees them as opportunities to learn and grow.

Protecting Sacred Boundaries

One of the Warrior's most important roles is to protect what is sacred—our values, our well-being, and our inner truth. Boundaries are the tools through which the Warrior fulfills this duty. For queer men, boundaries are essential in maintaining authenticity, navigating relationships, and safeguarding mental and emotional health.

Boundaries are not walls to isolate us from others but bridges that define how we engage with the world. A Warrior's boundaries are clear, firm, and rooted in self-respect.

Steps to establish and protect boundaries include:

1. **Know Your Worth**: Recognize what is non-negotiable for your well-being and growth.
2. **Communicate Clearly**: Articulate your boundaries with confidence and compassion.
3. **Enforce Boundaries Firmly**: Do not allow guilt or fear to compromise what you have established.
4. **Honor Others' Boundaries**: Respecting others' boundaries reinforces your own integrity.

By protecting sacred boundaries, the Warrior creates a space where authenticity and growth can flourish.

The Shadow Warrior

When distorted, the Warrior archetype becomes destructive rather than protective. The shadow Warrior can manifest in two primary forms:

- **The Aggressor**: Overwhelmed by fear or insecurity, this shadow seeks control through domination or violence. The Aggressor fights not for values but to protect an ego that feels threatened.
- **The Passive Warrior**: This shadow retreats from challenges, avoiding conflict or action out of fear or

self-doubt. The Passive Warrior abandons the sacred duty to protect and advocate for self and others.

Recognizing and addressing these shadow aspects is essential to embodying the Warrior in its highest form. The true Warrior acts with courage, clarity, and purpose, avoiding the pitfalls of aggression or passivity.

Taking Inspired Action

The Warrior thrives on action. However, this action is not reckless or impulsive; it is deliberate, guided by values and a clear sense of purpose. For queer men, taking inspired action often involves advocating for oneself and others, standing against injustice, and contributing to a world that celebrates diversity and inclusion.

Inspired action can take many forms:

- **Personal Growth**: Pursuing practices that strengthen mind, body, and spirit.
- **Advocacy**: Using your voice and actions to create positive change in your community.
- **Creative Expression**: Channeling the Warrior's energy into art, writing, or other forms of self-expression.
- **Acts of Service**: Supporting others in their journey, embodying the Warrior's role as a protector and ally.

By aligning action with intention, the Warrior transforms challenges into opportunities and obstacles into stepping stones.

The Warrior's Call

The Warrior archetype calls us to rise above fear, to act with integrity, and to protect what is sacred. For queer men, it offers the strength to live authentically, the courage to face adversity, and the discipline to create a life of purpose. The Warrior is not a lone fighter but a guardian of values, a builder of bridges, and a champion of truth.

As you step into the Warrior archetype, you become a beacon of resilience and empowerment. The path of the Warrior is not easy, but it is a path worth walking—a journey that leads not only to personal strength but to a life of meaning, connection, and impact. Will you answer the call?

The Magician: Wisdom and Transformation

The Magician archetype is the embodiment of wisdom, transformation, and spiritual intelligence. It represents the capacity to perceive deeper truths, access intuitive knowledge, and facilitate change within ourselves and the world around us. For queer men, the Magician offers a pathway to understanding the unique blend of masculine and feminine energies within, and the power to use this understanding for personal and collective growth.

The Magician is not bound by the surface of reality. Instead, this archetype delves into the unseen realms, exploring the mysteries of existence and harnessing them to bring about meaningful transformation. Whether through creativity, spiritual practices, or intellectual pursuits, the Magician channels insight into action, bridging the gap between knowledge and experience.

The Essence of the Magician

At its core, the Magician archetype is about awakening and utilizing higher intelligence—intellectual, emotional, and spiritual. It is the part of us that seeks understanding, not for dominance or control, but for enlightenment and empowerment.

The Magician is often associated with intuition, the ability to perceive beyond logic and reason. This intuitive wisdom allows us to recognize patterns, uncover hidden truths, and connect with the divine. For queer men, this archetype provides a vital tool for navigating a world that may not always understand or embrace our identity. By accessing the Magician's energy, we can tap into inner resources of resilience, creativity, and purpose.

Accessing Intuition

Intuition is one of the Magician's most powerful gifts. It is the ability to sense what lies beneath the surface, to understand without explanation, and to make decisions aligned with a deeper truth. For queer men, intuition can be a guiding force in navigating life's complexities, from relationships to self-expression.

Practices to strengthen intuition include:

1. **Meditation**: Quieting the mind to hear the subtle whispers of inner knowing.
2. **Journaling**: Reflecting on dreams, insights, and experiences to uncover patterns and meaning.
3. **Energy Work**: Exploring practices such as Reiki, breathwork, or chakra alignment to connect with intuitive energy.
4. **Trusting Your Gut**: Honoring instinctive feelings, even when they defy logic.

Intuition is not a magical gift reserved for a few; it is a natural ability that can be cultivated through practice and trust.

Embodying Spiritual Intelligence

Spiritual intelligence is the capacity to align with higher principles and values, to see beyond the material world, and to act with compassion and purpose. The Magician archetype embodies this intelligence, guiding us to live in harmony with the divine and to use our insights for the benefit of ourselves and others.

For queer men, spiritual intelligence involves embracing the duality of our existence—masculine and feminine, light and shadow—and integrating these aspects into a unified whole. This integration allows us to access our full potential, transforming personal struggles into opportunities for growth and self-discovery.

Ways to embody spiritual intelligence include:

1. **Study and Practice**: Explore spiritual traditions, philosophies, and practices that resonate with your path.
2. **Rituals and Ceremonies**: Create sacred moments to honor the divine within and around you.
3. **Community Engagement**: Share your wisdom and support others in their spiritual journeys.
4. **Creative Expression**: Channel spiritual insights into art, writing, or other forms of creativity.

The Transformative Power of the Magician

The Magician is a master of transformation, capable of turning pain into wisdom, obstacles into opportunities, and dreams into reality. This archetype reminds us that true change begins within and radiates outward. By aligning with the Magician's energy, we can unlock our potential to heal, grow, and inspire.

For queer men, this transformation often involves reclaiming the parts of ourselves that have been marginalized or suppressed. The Magician helps us see these aspects not as flaws but as sources of strength and creativity. Through this process, we become alchemists, turning the lead of our struggles into the gold of self-empowerment.

The Shadow Magician

When distorted, the Magician archetype can become manipulative, detached, or overly intellectual.

- **The Manipulative Magician**: Uses knowledge for personal gain, exploiting others or distorting the truth.
- **The Detached Magician**: Retreats into intellectualism or spirituality to avoid emotional connection or responsibility.

To embody the true essence of the Magician, we must remain grounded in integrity and compassion, using our insights to uplift rather than control.

Becoming the Magician

To step into the Magician archetype, we must cultivate both wisdom and humility. The Magician is a seeker and a teacher, continuously learning from life's experiences and sharing those lessons with others.

Steps to embody the Magician:

1. **Seek Knowledge**: Embrace curiosity and a commitment to lifelong learning.
2. **Practice Mindfulness**: Stay present and aware, attuned to the subtle energies around you.
3. **Take Inspired Action**: Use your insights to create positive change, both in your life and in the lives of others.
4. **Honor the Journey**: Recognize that transformation is a process, not a destination, and celebrate each step along the way.

The Magician's Legacy

The Magician archetype offers a vision of masculinity that is wise, compassionate, and transformative. For queer men, it provides a framework for accessing intuition, embodying spiritual intelligence, and creating a life of meaning and purpose.

As we embrace the Magician within, we become agents of change—not only for ourselves but for the world. The Magician's energy empowers us to bridge divides, heal wounds, and illuminate the path forward. In doing so, we claim our rightful place as creators, visionaries, and stewards of the divine.

Will you step into the role of the Magician and wield your power to transform?

The Lover: Sensuality and Connection

The Lover archetype is the heart of connection, sensuality, and emotional depth. It embodies the capacity to experience life fully, to revel in its beauty, and to form bonds that nurture and inspire. The Lover is the energy of passion—passion for life, for others, and for oneself. For queer men, the Lover represents not just romantic and physical love but also the profound act of self-love, which is essential for thriving in a world that may not always affirm our identity.

The Lover is both a source of joy and a mirror for the soul. It reminds us that to connect deeply with others, we must first connect deeply with ourselves. In celebrating intimacy, passion, and self-love, the Lover invites us to embrace our whole being—our desires, vulnerabilities, and dreams—and to find empowerment in our authenticity.

The Essence of the Lover

At its core, the Lover archetype is about experiencing life through the senses and the heart. It is the energy that draws us to beauty, whether in nature, art, relationships, or the moments of stillness where we feel most alive. The Lover teaches us to live fully, embracing the highs and lows of existence with openness and curiosity.

For queer men, the Lover is often a liberating force, encouraging us to break free from societal restrictions and to explore our identities and desires without shame. It is through the Lover that we find the courage to express ourselves authentically, to seek out meaningful connections, and to celebrate the richness of our unique experiences.

Celebrating Intimacy

Intimacy, at its deepest level, is about allowing ourselves to be seen and to see others fully. The Lover archetype fosters this vulnerability, creating spaces where we can connect without fear or pretense.

For queer men, intimacy can take many forms:

- **Romantic and Physical Intimacy**: Building relationships that honor mutual respect, trust, and shared passion.
- **Emotional Intimacy**: Sharing our thoughts, feelings, and dreams with others, creating bonds that go beyond the surface.
- **Spiritual Intimacy**: Connecting with others on a soul level, sharing a sense of purpose and meaning.

Cultivating intimacy requires openness and courage. It challenges us to let go of defenses and embrace the risk of connection, knowing that true intimacy enriches and transforms our lives.

Honoring Passion

The Lover archetype celebrates passion—the spark that ignites our creativity, fuels our pursuits, and connects us to others. Passion is not limited to romantic relationships; it is the force that drives us to live fully and to pursue what makes us feel alive.

For queer men, passion often involves exploring parts of ourselves that have been suppressed or marginalized. The Lover encourages us to rediscover our desires, whether they relate to art, relationships, activism, or personal growth. By embracing our passions, we tap into a wellspring of energy and purpose that enhances every aspect of our lives.

Practical ways to honor passion include:

1. **Creative Expression**: Channeling your emotions and inspirations into art, writing, music, or other forms of creativity.
2. **Exploration**: Trying new experiences, relationships, or hobbies that spark curiosity and excitement.
3. **Connection**: Sharing your passions with others, building communities of like-minded individuals.
4. **Presence**: Fully immersing yourself in the present moment, savoring life's pleasures without distraction.

Cultivating Self-Love

Self-love is the foundation of the Lover archetype. It is the act of accepting and valuing ourselves as we are, without judgment or comparison. For queer men, self-love is a radical and transformative practice, offering healing from the wounds of rejection, shame, or marginalization.

Cultivating self-love involves:

1. **Acknowledging Worth**: Recognizing that your identity and experiences are valid and valuable.
2. **Practicing Compassion**: Treating yourself with kindness, especially during moments of struggle or self-doubt.
3. **Nurturing the Body**: Caring for your physical health through rest, movement, and nourishment.
4. **Affirming Your Desires**: Embracing your wants and needs without guilt or apology.

Self-love is not selfish; it is the foundation for healthy relationships and a fulfilling life. By loving ourselves, we create a ripple effect of positivity that extends to everyone we encounter.

The Shadow Lover

Like all archetypes, the Lover has a shadow side. When out of balance, the Lover can become consumed by excess or avoidance:

- **The Addicted Lover**: Overindulges in pleasure, losing sight of boundaries and purpose.
- **The Disconnected Lover**: Avoids intimacy, retreating into isolation or emotional numbness.

To embody the true essence of the Lover, we must integrate its energy with the discipline of the Warrior and the wisdom of the Magician. This balance allows us to celebrate life's pleasures while remaining grounded and purposeful.

The Lover's Role in the Collective

The Lover archetype is not only about personal fulfillment; it also plays a vital role in fostering connection and compassion within the broader community. By embracing the Lover, queer men can become beacons of authenticity, creating spaces where others feel safe to express themselves and form meaningful bonds.

The Lover's energy has the power to heal divides, inspire creativity, and nurture a sense of belonging. In a world that often values productivity over connection, the Lover reminds us of the importance of relationships, joy, and shared humanity.

Becoming the Lover

To embody the Lover archetype, we must embrace the full spectrum of our emotions, desires, and connections. This journey involves celebrating our sensuality, honoring our passions, and cultivating deep, authentic relationships with ourselves and others.

Steps to embody the Lover:

1. **Celebrate Sensuality**: Explore ways to connect with your senses, whether through touch, taste, sound, or movement.

2. **Deepen Connections**: Invest time and energy in relationships that bring joy and fulfillment.
3. **Practice Gratitude**: Focus on the beauty and abundance in your life, cultivating a sense of appreciation.
4. **Prioritize Pleasure**: Make time for activities and experiences that bring you joy, without guilt or justification.

The Lover's Gift

The Lover archetype offers the gift of connection—connection to self, others, and the world. It teaches us to live with passion, to embrace intimacy, and to honor the unique beauty of our existence. For queer men, the Lover represents the power of authenticity and the joy of living fully, even in the face of challenges.

By stepping into the Lover's energy, we claim our right to experience life's pleasures and to build relationships that inspire and sustain us. The Lover invites us to see the world through the lens of love, reminding us that connection is the essence of life. Will you open your heart to the Lover within?

Part 3: Integrating Masculine and Feminine Energies

Shiva and Shakti: The Union of Energies

The integration of masculine and feminine energies is one of the most profound and empowering journeys we can undertake. For queer men, this balance is not only a natural part of our identity but also a source of immense strength and creativity. At the heart of this integration lies the ancient concept of **Shiva**

and Shakti, a duality that represents consciousness and creation, stillness and movement, masculine and feminine. Together, they reveal the divine interplay necessary for wholeness and empowerment.

The Archetypes of Shiva and Shakti

In Hindu tradition, Shiva represents the masculine principle of consciousness. He is the stillness, the observer, the one who gives form and direction to creation. Shakti, in contrast, is the feminine principle of energy. She is the movement, the force of creation, the dynamic energy that brings ideas into reality.

Individually, Shiva and Shakti are incomplete. Shiva, without Shakti, is dormant and inert—a potential that remains unrealized. Shakti, without Shiva, is chaotic and aimless—energy without structure or purpose. It is only in their union that action, movement, and creation become possible. Together, they form **Ardhanarishvara**, the androgynous deity that embodies the perfect balance of masculine and feminine energies.

For queer men, the story of Shiva and Shakti offers a powerful metaphor for integrating our own dualities. It invites us to embrace both the stillness and the movement within, recognizing that true empowerment lies in the harmony between the two.

Consciousness and Creation

The balance of Shiva and Shakti represents the interplay between consciousness (masculine) and creation (feminine).

- **Consciousness (Shiva):** This is the ability to observe, reflect, and provide direction. It is the grounded energy that allows us to make decisions with clarity and purpose.
- **Creation (Shakti):** This is the force of action, creativity, and passion. It is the vibrant energy that brings our ideas and desires into tangible form.

For queer men, these energies are often already present in dynamic interplay. We navigate the world with the precision of consciousness while infusing it with the creative energy of transformation. By consciously balancing these forces, we can channel our unique strengths to create a life that is both grounded and inspired.

Balancing Masculine and Feminine Energies

To achieve balance, we must honor both our masculine and feminine aspects, recognizing that neither is superior to the other. This requires moving beyond societal conditioning, which often equates masculinity with strength and femininity with weakness. Instead, we see these energies as complementary forces, each essential to our wholeness.

Practical Ways to Balance These Energies:

1. **Reflective Practices (Shiva):**
    -   Meditate to cultivate stillness and awareness.
    -   Journal to clarify your thoughts and emotions.
    -   Set intentional goals to direct your energy with purpose.
2. **Creative Practices (Shakti):**
    -   Dance, paint, or engage in other forms of artistic expression.
    -   Explore your passions through experimentation and play.
    -   Embrace spontaneity, allowing yourself to move with the flow of life.
3. **Integration Practices:**
    -   Yoga: Combines breath, movement, and mindfulness, balancing stillness and action.
    -   Rituals: Honor both energies by creating ceremonies that incorporate reflection and celebration.
    -   Nature Connection: Spend time in environments that inspire both tranquility (mountains, forests) and vibrancy (oceans, bustling gardens).

Empowerment Through Integration

The integration of masculine and feminine energies is not just a personal journey; it is an act of empowerment. By harmonizing these forces, queer men can transcend societal expectations and create new paradigms for living authentically. This integration allows us to:

- **Lead with Compassion:** Combining the decisiveness of Shiva with the nurturing energy of Shakti.
- **Create with Purpose:** Using Shakti's creativity to manifest ideas guided by Shiva's clarity.
- **Transform Challenges:** Drawing on both strength and adaptability to navigate obstacles.

When these energies are in balance, we experience a sense of flow and alignment. Our actions feel purposeful, our relationships are enriched, and our inner world becomes a source of resilience and joy.

Shiva and Shakti in Everyday Life

The interplay of Shiva and Shakti is not limited to grand spiritual moments; it is a daily practice. Every decision, every action, every moment holds the potential for balance. Consider these examples:

- **In Relationships:** Balance the need for emotional vulnerability (Shakti) with the stability of clear communication (Shiva).
- **In Work:** Pair creativity and innovation (Shakti) with discipline and focus (Shiva).
- **In Self-Care:** Alternate between restful introspection (Shiva) and energizing activities (Shakti).

By weaving these energies into our daily lives, we cultivate a dynamic equilibrium that supports our growth and well-being.

The Queer Empowerment of Shiva and Shakti

For queer men, the union of Shiva and Shakti is especially meaningful. It affirms that our existence is not a deviation but a reflection of divine balance. As individuals who often embody both masculine and feminine energies, we are uniquely positioned to model this integration for others.

This empowerment is not about fitting into predefined roles but about creating new ones. By embracing the duality within, we redefine strength, love, and creativity on our own terms. We become leaders and healers, bridging gaps between tradition and innovation, between the masculine and the feminine, and between consciousness and creation.

The Invitation to Balance

The story of Shiva and Shakti invites us to see ourselves as whole, dynamic beings capable of infinite potential. It reminds us that the path to empowerment lies not in choosing one energy over the other but in embracing both with equal reverence.

As you explore this balance in your own life, consider the ways in which Shiva and Shakti already manifest within you. What parts of yourself need stillness? Where can you invite more energy and creation? The answers to these questions will guide you toward a life of greater harmony, authenticity, and empowerment.

The union of Shiva and Shakti is not just a spiritual concept—it is a lived experience, an ongoing journey toward wholeness. Will you step into this sacred dance and claim the full power of your integrated self?

Healing the Feminine Within

Nurturing Compassion, Creativity, and Vulnerability

The feminine within each of us is a wellspring of compassion, creativity, and emotional depth. It is the energy that allows us to connect with others, to create beauty from chaos, and to embrace vulnerability as a source of strength. For queer men, healing the feminine within is a transformative journey—one that involves reclaiming aspects of ourselves that have been suppressed, marginalized, or misunderstood. It is a process of nurturing our capacity to feel deeply, to care for ourselves and others, and to create a life of authenticity and fulfillment.

Understanding the Feminine Within

The feminine energy within us is not about gender but about qualities and expressions that exist in balance with the masculine. It encompasses traits such as:

- **Compassion**: The ability to care deeply for oneself and others.
- **Creativity**: The capacity to bring new ideas, emotions, and experiences into being.
- **Vulnerability**: The courage to embrace emotions and authentic connections.

In many cultures, the feminine has been undervalued, often viewed as weak or secondary to the masculine. This cultural bias has led to the suppression of feminine traits in men, creating imbalances in our personal and collective lives. For queer men, this suppression is often compounded by societal expectations that dismiss our unique blend of masculine and feminine energies.

Healing the feminine within is not about rejecting the masculine but about integrating these energies to create wholeness. It is about honoring the parts of ourselves that feel, nurture, and imagine, and recognizing that these qualities are not weaknesses but profound strengths.

Nurturing Compassion

Compassion is the heart of the feminine. It is the ability to see and respond to the needs of others, to extend kindness and understanding, and to cultivate deep connections. For queer men, compassion begins with self-acceptance—acknowledging our own worth and extending grace to ourselves.

Practical ways to nurture compassion include:

1. **Practice Self-Compassion**: Speak to yourself with kindness, especially during moments of self-doubt or struggle.
2. **Engage in Acts of Service**: Offer your time or resources to support others, creating a ripple effect of kindness.
3. **Listen Actively**: Foster deeper connections by truly hearing and empathizing with others.

Compassion is not only a gift to others but also a healing force for ourselves. By opening our hearts, we create spaces of safety and connection where growth can flourish.

Cultivating Creativity

Creativity is a defining characteristic of the feminine within. It is the ability to take inspiration and transform it into something tangible, whether it is art, relationships, or innovative ideas. For queer men, creativity often becomes a tool for self-expression, allowing us to explore and communicate our identities in unique ways.

Steps to cultivate creativity:

1. **Explore New Mediums**: Experiment with writing, painting, music, or other forms of artistic expression.
2. **Embrace Playfulness**: Approach life with curiosity and a sense of adventure, allowing yourself to try new things without fear of failure.
3. **Create Rituals**: Develop routines that inspire creativity, such as journaling in the morning or taking walks in nature.

Creativity is not limited to artistic pursuits; it is a way of approaching life. By embracing our creative potential, we not only enrich our own lives but also contribute to the beauty and diversity of the world.

Embracing Vulnerability

Vulnerability is one of the most misunderstood aspects of the feminine. Far from being a weakness, vulnerability is the courage to be authentic, to show our true selves, and to form genuine connections. For queer men, embracing vulnerability often involves overcoming societal messages that equate openness with fragility.

Steps to embrace vulnerability:

1. **Acknowledge Your Emotions**: Allow yourself to feel and express a full range of emotions, from joy to sadness.
2. **Practice Authenticity**: Share your thoughts and feelings honestly, even when it feels uncomfortable.
3. **Build Trust**: Surround yourself with people who value and respect your openness, creating spaces where vulnerability feels safe.

Vulnerability is a bridge to deeper relationships and a richer inner life. It allows us to connect not only with others but also with the parts of ourselves that we may have hidden or ignored.

Healing Wounds of the Feminine

For many queer men, the feminine within has been wounded by cultural stigma, personal rejection, or internalized shame. These wounds can manifest as fear of intimacy, creative blockages, or difficulty expressing emotions. Healing these wounds requires patience, self-awareness, and a commitment to growth.

Steps to heal the feminine within:

1. **Identify the Wounds**: Reflect on moments where your feminine energy was dismissed or devalued.
2. **Reclaim Your Power**: Affirm the value of compassion, creativity, and vulnerability in your life.
3. **Seek Support**: Work with a therapist, mentor, or supportive community to process and heal these wounds.

Healing is not a linear process, but every step toward honoring the feminine within brings us closer to wholeness.

Integrating Masculine and Feminine Energies

Healing the feminine within is part of a larger journey of integrating masculine and feminine energies. This integration allows us to embody the full spectrum of who we are, creating balance and harmony in our lives. When the feminine is nurtured, it enriches the masculine, adding depth, empathy, and creativity to our strength and focus.

The Power of the Feminine Within

The feminine within each of us is a source of profound power—not the power to dominate but the power to connect, create, and heal. For queer men, this energy is a vital part of our identity, offering a path to authenticity and empowerment.

By nurturing compassion, cultivating creativity, and embracing vulnerability, we honor the feminine within and create a life that is rich in meaning and connection. The journey to healing the feminine is not just about reclaiming parts of ourselves; it is about stepping into a fuller, more vibrant expression of who we are.

Will you embrace this journey and celebrate the power of the feminine within?

Healing the Masculine Wounds

Overcoming Toxic Conditioning and Reclaiming Authentic Masculinity

Masculinity, in its essence, is a force of strength, purpose, and protection. Yet, for many queer men, the journey to embrace authentic masculinity has been hindered by societal expectations, cultural stigma, and personal experiences of rejection or harm. These pressures often create wounds that distort our relationship with masculinity, leaving us questioning its role in our identity. Healing the masculine wounds involves breaking free from toxic conditioning, reclaiming our right to define masculinity on our terms, and embodying its truest, most empowering form.

Understanding the Wounds of Masculinity

Masculine wounds are the result of a lifetime of messages, experiences, and cultural expectations that diminish or distort our understanding of what it means to be a man. These wounds often stem from:

- **Toxic Masculinity**: A cultural framework that equates masculinity with dominance, aggression, and emotional repression.
- **Internalized Shame**: Feelings of inadequacy or failure to meet societal standards of manhood.
- **Rejection and Marginalization**: Experiences of exclusion or judgment for expressing masculinity in ways that deviate from heteronormative norms.

For queer men, these wounds are often compounded by the challenges of navigating a world that does not fully embrace or understand us. They manifest as fear, self-doubt, or a disconnection from our own power. Healing begins with acknowledging these wounds and recognizing that they are not reflections of our worth but symptoms of a broken cultural system.

Breaking Free from Toxic Conditioning

Toxic conditioning teaches us that masculinity must conform to narrow definitions—stoicism, physical dominance, and emotional detachment. These messages create a false ideal that alienates queer men and denies the full spectrum of masculine expression.

Steps to Overcome Toxic Conditioning

1. **Recognize Harmful Beliefs**: Reflect on the societal messages you've internalized about masculinity and how they may limit you.
2. **Challenge Stereotypes**: Actively question and reject the notion that masculinity must be defined by dominance, aggression, or suppression of emotion.
3. **Redefine Masculinity**: Embrace a vision of masculinity that values authenticity, empathy, and strength in vulnerability.
4. **Seek Role Models**: Look to individuals who embody positive and diverse expressions of masculinity, offering inspiration and validation.

Breaking free from toxic conditioning allows us to reclaim the masculine on our terms, creating space for growth, authenticity, and empowerment.

Reclaiming Authentic Masculinity

Authentic masculinity is not about conforming to societal expectations but about aligning with the traits and values that resonate with our true selves. It honors both strength and sensitivity, leadership and collaboration, action and reflection.

Core Elements of Authentic Masculinity

- **Strength**: Not as dominance, but as resilience, self-assurance, and the ability to uplift others.
- **Courage**: The willingness to be vulnerable, to stand up for your truth, and to take meaningful action.
- **Integrity**: Aligning your actions with your values, fostering trust and respect.
- **Empathy**: Understanding and valuing the experiences and feelings of others.

Authentic masculinity is fluid and dynamic, adapting to the needs of the moment while remaining rooted in self-awareness and purpose.

Healing Through Self-Compassion

Healing the masculine wounds requires us to approach ourselves with compassion. Many of us have internalized shame for failing to meet societal ideals of masculinity. This shame is not ours to carry, and releasing it begins with recognizing our inherent worth.

Practices for Self-Compassion

1. **Acknowledge Your Struggles**: Understand that your experiences and wounds are valid, and that healing is a journey.
2. **Forgive Yourself**: Release guilt or regret for conforming to or resisting societal expectations in the past.
3. **Celebrate Your Identity**: Embrace your unique expression of masculinity as a source of strength and beauty.
4. **Seek Support**: Connect with communities or mentors who affirm and support your healing process.

Self-compassion allows us to honor our journey without judgment, creating the foundation for lasting growth and transformation.

Transforming Pain into Power

Our wounds, when acknowledged and addressed, become sources of wisdom and strength. The process of healing transforms pain into power, teaching us resilience, empathy, and self-awareness. For queer men, this transformation often involves:

- **Embracing Vulnerability**: Recognizing that openness and emotional expression are signs of strength, not weakness.
- **Building Community**: Forming connections with others who understand and validate your journey.

- **Advocating for Change**: Using your experiences to inspire and empower others, fostering a culture that values authentic masculinity.

The Role of Ritual in Healing

Rituals provide a powerful framework for healing masculine wounds. They allow us to symbolically release old patterns, affirm new intentions, and connect with the divine masculine within.

Examples of Healing Rituals

1. **Release Ceremony**: Write down limiting beliefs about masculinity and burn them as a symbolic act of letting go.
2. **Affirmation Practice**: Create daily affirmations that celebrate your authentic masculinity.
3. **Nature Connection**: Spend time in environments that inspire strength and renewal, such as forests or mountains.

Through ritual, we can anchor our healing process in meaningful, transformative actions.

Moving Forward: A New Vision of Masculinity

Healing the masculine wounds is not about discarding masculinity but about reclaiming it in its truest form. It is about honoring the parts of ourselves that are strong and protective while also nurturing our capacity for connection and compassion.

For queer men, this journey is a radical act of self-love and empowerment. It is a rejection of societal expectations that limit us and an embrace of the expansive potential within. By healing our wounds, we create a new vision of masculinity—one that is inclusive, authentic, and transformative.

The Invitation to Heal

The journey to heal the masculine wounds is both personal and collective. As individuals, we reclaim our power and purpose. As a community, we redefine what it means to be a man in a way that honors diversity and authenticity.

Will you step into this journey and reclaim the fullness of your masculinity? The path may be challenging, but it is one that leads to freedom, empowerment, and a deeper connection with yourself and the world.

Part 4: Pathways to Empowerment

The Spiritual Warrior: Overcoming Shadows

The Spiritual Warrior is a central figure in the journey toward empowerment, embodying the courage and discipline necessary to confront and transcend the shadows that cloud our lives. These shadows may arise from personal fears, unresolved traumas, or societal expectations that stifle authenticity. For queer men, the path of the Spiritual Warrior is particularly transformative, offering a way to face internal and external challenges with strength, resilience, and purpose.

Understanding the Shadow

In Jungian psychology, the shadow represents the parts of ourselves that we reject, suppress, or deny. These aspects can include fears, insecurities, desires, or behaviors that we perceive as undesirable or incompatible with our self-image. While the shadow is often seen as negative, it also contains hidden potential and unclaimed power.

For queer men, shadows frequently emerge from the tension between societal expectations and personal identity. These may include:

- **Internalized Shame**: Feelings of inadequacy or unworthiness due to cultural stigma.
- **Fear of Rejection**: Avoidance of authenticity to gain acceptance or avoid judgment.
- **Suppressed Desires**: A reluctance to embrace parts of ourselves that challenge norms or expectations.

Acknowledging and integrating the shadow is a key step in personal growth. The Spiritual Warrior approaches this task with honesty, courage, and compassion, transforming the shadow from a source of fear into a wellspring of strength and wisdom.

Facing Personal Shadows

To overcome personal shadows, the Spiritual Warrior employs techniques that foster self-awareness, acceptance, and transformation.

Techniques for Facing Personal Shadows

1. **Shadow Work**: Engage in practices that uncover and explore hidden aspects of yourself, such as journaling or guided meditations. Reflect on moments of emotional discomfort or judgment to identify underlying fears or beliefs.
2. **Self-Compassion**: Approach your shadows with kindness and understanding, recognizing that they are part of your humanity.
3. **Inner Dialogue**: Engage in conversations with your shadow self, asking what it needs and how it can be integrated into your life.
4. **Visualization**: Imagine yourself embracing and transforming your shadow, turning its energy into a source of strength.

By facing personal shadows, the Spiritual Warrior reclaims power that was previously locked away, creating space for growth and authenticity.

Confronting Societal Shadows

Societal shadows are the collective fears, prejudices, and injustices that shape the world we live in. For queer men, these often include systemic discrimination, cultural stigmas, and rigid gender roles. Confronting these shadows requires both personal resilience and collective action.

Techniques for Confronting Societal Shadows

1. **Education and Awareness**: Learn about the historical and cultural forces that perpetuate societal shadows. Knowledge is a powerful tool for dismantling ignorance and fear.
2. **Advocacy**: Use your voice and actions to challenge injustice and promote inclusivity, whether through activism, mentorship, or everyday interactions.
3. **Community Building**: Create and participate in supportive networks that empower individuals and foster understanding.
4. **Model Authenticity**: Live as a visible example of truth and courage, inspiring others to challenge societal norms and embrace their identities.

The Spiritual Warrior understands that confronting societal shadows is not just about resistance but also about creating a vision for a more inclusive and compassionate world.

Overcoming Fear

Fear is one of the most pervasive shadows, often preventing us from taking meaningful action or embracing our true selves. The Spiritual Warrior does not seek to eliminate fear but to transform it into a source of strength.

Techniques for Overcoming Fear

1. **Name Your Fear**: Clearly identify what you are afraid of and why. Naming fear reduces its power and makes it more manageable.
2. **Reframe Fear as Growth**: View fear as an opportunity to grow and expand, rather than as a barrier.
3. **Take Small Steps**: Break down challenges into smaller, manageable actions that build confidence and momentum.
4. **Anchor in Purpose**: Remind yourself of your deeper motivations and values, using them as a compass to guide you through fear.

Fear is a natural part of growth, but the Spiritual Warrior refuses to let it dictate their life. By confronting fear, they step into their full power and potential.

The Role of Ritual in Shadow Work

Rituals are a powerful tool for the Spiritual Warrior, providing structure and meaning to the process of overcoming shadows.

Examples of Shadow Work Rituals

1. **Release Ceremony**: Write down fears, judgments, or limiting beliefs on paper and burn them as a symbolic act of letting go.
2. **Mirror Meditation**: Sit in front of a mirror, gaze into your own eyes, and speak affirmations that acknowledge and integrate your shadow.
3. **Visualization Journey**: Imagine yourself as a warrior entering a dark forest (the shadow) and emerging with treasures (wisdom and strength).
4. **Sacred Circle**: Create a physical or symbolic circle to hold space for your shadow work, honoring the process as sacred and transformative.

Through ritual, the Spiritual Warrior creates a bridge between intention and action, grounding their journey in purpose and reverence.

Transcending the Shadows

Overcoming shadows is not about erasing them but about integrating them into a balanced and empowered self. The Spiritual Warrior understands that shadows contain valuable lessons and potential. By embracing these parts of themselves, they become whole.

For queer men, this journey is an act of radical self-acceptance and liberation. It is a rejection of societal narratives that seek to diminish us and a celebration of our capacity for growth and transformation. The Spiritual Warrior transcends the shadows not by avoiding them but by walking through them with courage and clarity.

Empowerment Through the Spiritual Warrior

The path of the Spiritual Warrior is one of resilience, authenticity, and empowerment. By facing and transcending personal and societal shadows, we reclaim our right to live fully and freely. We become leaders, healers, and visionaries, not in spite of our shadows but because of them.

As you walk this path, remember that the shadows are not obstacles but opportunities for transformation. They are invitations to step into your power and to create a life of meaning and purpose.

Will you answer the call of the Spiritual Warrior and face your shadows with courage? The journey is not easy, but it is the path to freedom, strength, and true empowerment.

The Alchemical Process of Transformation

Turning Pain into Power Through Rituals and Mindfulness

Transformation is at the heart of the human journey, and for queer men, it often involves navigating pain to uncover strength, wisdom, and empowerment. The alchemical process of transformation is a metaphor for this journey, inspired by the ancient practice of alchemy—turning base metals into gold. In this context, alchemy represents the ability to transform emotional, spiritual, and societal struggles into sources of power, purpose, and self-realization.

Rituals and mindfulness provide the tools for this transformation, offering structure and focus as we confront pain, release old patterns, and step into a new version of ourselves. By approaching transformation as an alchemical process, we honor both the difficulty and the beauty of change.

Understanding the Alchemical Process

Alchemy operates on the principle that transformation is a multi-step journey requiring intention, focus, and inner work. In spiritual alchemy, this process often includes three key stages:

1. **Calcination (Burning Away)**: The breaking down of old identities, beliefs, and attachments that no longer serve us.
2. **Dissolution (Releasing)**: Surrendering to the process of change, allowing emotions and resistance to flow and dissipate.
3. **Coagulation (Rebirth)**: The creation of something new and authentic from the ashes of what was released.

For queer men, this process reflects the journey of reclaiming identity and power in a world that often imposes limiting narratives on who we can be. Each stage offers an opportunity to confront pain, embrace vulnerability, and emerge stronger and more aligned with our true selves.

Turning Pain Into Power

Pain, while challenging, is also an invitation to grow. The alchemical process teaches us to view pain not as a punishment but as a catalyst for transformation. When we approach pain with mindfulness and intention, we can extract its lessons and use it as fuel for empowerment.

Steps to Transform Pain:

1. **Acknowledge the Pain**: Fully recognize and name your pain without judgment. Allow yourself to feel it, rather than suppressing or avoiding it.
2. **Reflect on Its Origin**: Explore where the pain comes from—whether it's rooted in past experiences, limiting beliefs, or societal pressures.
3. **Extract the Lesson**: Ask yourself what the pain is teaching you. What strength or insight can you gain from it?
4. **Release What No Longer Serves**: Through ritual or mindfulness, let go of the aspects of pain that hold you back.

Pain can be a teacher, but it need not define us. By consciously engaging with it, we reclaim power that was once lost or hidden.

The Role of Rituals in Transformation

Rituals are a cornerstone of the alchemical process, providing symbolic and practical frameworks for releasing the old and welcoming the new. They ground our transformation in action, creating sacred spaces where healing can occur.

Transformative Rituals:

1. **Burning Ceremony**: Write down thoughts, beliefs, or emotions you want to release and burn the paper as a symbol of letting go.
2. **Water Cleansing Ritual**: Use water, such as a bath or a flowing stream, to wash away pain and renew your energy. Visualize the water carrying away what no longer serves you.
3. **Rebirth Meditation**: Envision yourself emerging from a cocoon or stepping into a golden light, transformed and empowered.
4. **Sacred Object Ritual**: Infuse a meaningful object, such as a crystal or piece of jewelry, with the intention of your transformation. Carry it as a reminder of your power.

Rituals create a tangible connection between your inner work and the external world, reinforcing the changes you are making.

The Power of Mindfulness

Mindfulness complements rituals by fostering a deeper awareness of the present moment and your internal landscape.

It allows you to engage with the alchemical process consciously and compassionately, staying connected to your intentions even in moments of discomfort.

Mindfulness Practices for Transformation:

1. **Body Scan Meditation**: Tune into physical sensations, identifying where pain or resistance resides in your body. Visualize releasing tension and inviting healing energy.
2. **Breathwork**: Use intentional breathing to calm your mind, release emotions, and cultivate focus.
3. **Gratitude Practice**: Reflect on what the process of transformation has taught you, finding gratitude even in the challenges.
4. **Affirmations**: Speak words of empowerment, such as "I am transforming my pain into power" or "I release the old and embrace the new."

Mindfulness anchors you in the present, helping you navigate each stage of transformation with clarity and grace.

The Rebirth: Emerging Empowered

The final stage of the alchemical process is rebirth, where pain is transmuted into power and authenticity. This is the moment of integration, where you step into a new version of yourself—one that honors your journey and embodies your strengths.

Signs of Transformation:

- A greater sense of purpose and alignment with your values.
- Increased resilience and confidence in facing challenges.
- A deeper connection to yourself and others.
- The ability to let go of the past and embrace the present.

Rebirth is not a single event but an ongoing process. Each time you confront and transform pain, you expand your capacity for growth and empowerment.

Embracing the Alchemical Path

The alchemical process of transformation is a powerful framework for navigating life's challenges and discovering your potential. It teaches us that pain is not the end but the beginning—a catalyst for change that, when met with intention and courage, reveals our inner gold.

For queer men, this process is particularly liberating. It allows us to break free from societal constraints, heal wounds of the past, and reclaim our identities as creators, leaders, and visionaries. Through rituals and mindfulness, we forge a path of empowerment that honors both our struggles and our triumphs.

The journey of transformation is not always easy, but it is always worthwhile. Will you step into the alchemical process and turn your pain into power? The choice is yours, and the rewards are infinite.

The Role of Ritual in Queer Masculinity

Designing and Embracing Personal Rites of Passage

Rituals have long been a cornerstone of human experience, providing structure, meaning, and connection to life's most significant transitions. For queer men, rituals hold the potential to honor our unique experiences and affirm our identities in a world that often excludes us from traditional rites of passage.

By creating and embracing personal rituals, we reclaim the power to define masculinity on our own terms, celebrating our journeys and fostering deeper connection with ourselves, our communities, and the divine.

Why Rituals Matter in Queer Masculinity

Rituals serve as transformative acts that mark important milestones, transitions, and intentions. For queer men, they can:

- **Affirm Identity**: Providing spaces to honor our individuality and celebrate our uniqueness.
- **Create Community**: Building bonds with others through shared symbolic actions.
- **Foster Growth**: Offering opportunities to reflect on challenges and step into new roles.
- **Honor the Sacred**: Connecting us to higher principles, the divine, or our inner wisdom.

Traditional masculinity often emphasizes rigid rites of passage—such as military service, fatherhood, or professional achievements—that may not resonate with queer experiences. By designing personal rituals, we create meaningful ceremonies that reflect our values, strengths, and truths.

Designing Personal Rites of Passage

A personal rite of passage is a ritual that marks a significant moment or transformation in your life. It can be as simple or elaborate as you desire, but its power lies in its intentionality and relevance to your unique journey.

Steps to Create a Personal Rite of Passage:

1. **Identify the Transition**: Reflect on a specific moment, milestone, or transformation you want to honor. This could be a coming-out anniversary, a career change, a relationship milestone, or a period of personal growth.
2. **Define the Meaning**: Ask yourself what this moment represents. What are you letting go of, and what are you stepping into?
3. **Choose Symbolic Actions**: Select actions, objects, or practices that symbolize the transformation. Examples include lighting a candle, wearing specific clothing, or writing and reciting a declaration.
4. **Set the Stage**: Create a physical or symbolic space for the ritual. This might be a sacred circle, a natural location, or a quiet room in your home.
5. **Include Community (Optional)**: Invite supportive friends, loved ones, or a spiritual community to witness or participate in your ritual. Their presence can add depth and meaning.
6. **Conclude with Intention**: End the ritual with an action or statement that solidifies your transformation, such as planting a seed, releasing an object, or speaking an affirmation.

By designing a ritual that reflects your values and experiences, you take ownership of your transformation and create a lasting memory of empowerment.

Examples of Rites of Passage for Queer Men

1. **Coming Out Ceremony**
   - Celebrate the courage and authenticity of coming out by lighting a candle to symbolize stepping into your truth. Share your story with supportive friends or write a letter to your younger self, affirming your journey.

2. **Embracing Queer Masculinity**
   - Honor your unique blend of masculine and feminine energies with a ritual that includes both grounded actions (e.g., standing firmly, reciting affirmations of strength) and fluid expressions (e.g., dance or creative movement).

3. **Releasing Past Pain**
   - Create a ritual to let go of old wounds or limiting beliefs. Write them down and burn the paper in a fire-safe container, symbolizing release and renewal.

4. **Stepping Into Leadership**
   - Mark a transition into a role of leadership or advocacy with a ceremony that includes symbols of power, such as wearing a crown, holding a staff, or invoking the King archetype.

5. **Celebrating Love**
   - Honor a meaningful relationship with a shared ritual, such as exchanging symbolic objects, planting a tree together, or creating a shared piece of art.

Incorporating Rituals into Daily Life

While rites of passage mark significant moments, rituals can also be woven into everyday life to support and affirm queer masculinity.

Daily and Weekly Ritual Ideas:

- **Morning Grounding Practice**: Begin each day by lighting a candle, meditating, or reciting an affirmation that connects you to your masculine and feminine energies.
- **Creative Expression**: Dedicate time each week to an artistic or expressive activity that celebrates your identity.
- **Connection Ritual**: Spend time connecting with loved ones, whether through a shared meal, meaningful conversation, or a spiritual practice.
- **Reflection Practice**: End your day by journaling about what you've learned, released, or celebrated.

These small acts create a sense of continuity and intention, reminding you of your power and purpose.

Healing Through Rituals

For queer men, rituals also serve as tools for healing. They provide spaces to process grief, release shame, and reclaim parts of ourselves that have been suppressed or marginalized.

Healing Ritual Ideas:

- **Grief Ceremony**: Create a sacred space to honor losses—whether personal, relational, or societal. Speak your feelings aloud or write them down and release them into water or fire.
- **Self-Love Ritual**: Dedicate time to care for your body and soul, such as taking a ritual bath, adorning yourself with symbols of beauty and strength, or meditating on your worth.
- **Reconnection Ceremony**: If you've felt disconnected from your queer identity, design a ritual to reconnect, such as reading queer literature, creating art that celebrates your journey, or visiting a place of significance to your community.

Rituals not only mark transitions but also provide pathways for integration, helping us move forward with clarity and purpose.

The Empowerment of Ritual in Queer Masculinity

Rituals allow queer men to step into their power, affirm their journeys, and create meaning in a world that often denies it.

They provide tools to celebrate, heal, and connect, offering pathways to a more authentic and empowered life.

By designing and embracing personal rituals, we reclaim control over our narratives and honor the fullness of our experiences. We redefine masculinity not as a rigid set of rules but as a dynamic, inclusive expression of strength, compassion, and creativity.

Will you embrace the power of ritual to transform and affirm your journey? The tools are in your hands, and the possibilities are infinite.

Embodied Masculinity: Physical Practices for Empowerment

Yoga, Meditation, and Somatic Experiences to Anchor Empowerment

Masculinity, when fully embodied, transcends societal expectations and becomes an integrated expression of strength, resilience, and presence. For queer men, the journey to embodied masculinity involves anchoring empowerment not just in the mind or emotions but in the body itself. Physical practices such as yoga, meditation, and somatic experiences provide tools to ground this energy, fostering a deep connection between the body, mind, and spirit. These practices help release stored tension, cultivate inner strength, and align physical actions with authentic masculinity.

The Importance of Embodiment in Masculinity

Embodiment means living fully in the body, experiencing life through the physical self rather than merely through thoughts or emotions. For queer men, this connection is particularly transformative, as many of us have experienced disconnection from our bodies due to societal pressures, shame, or trauma.

Embodied masculinity allows us to:

- **Reclaim Power**: Grounding in the body enhances confidence and a sense of control over one's life.
- **Release Emotional Blockages**: Physical practices help process and release emotions stored in the body.
- **Cultivate Presence**: Being fully present in the body fosters authenticity and connection in relationships.
- **Anchor Resilience**: A strong physical foundation supports mental and emotional well-being.

Yoga for Embodied Masculinity

Yoga is a holistic practice that integrates physical movement, breathwork, and mindfulness, making it an ideal tool for cultivating embodied masculinity. It strengthens the body while fostering flexibility, balance, and a deeper connection to the self.

Yoga Poses to Cultivate Masculine Energy

1. **Warrior Pose (Virabhadrasana I, II, III)**
   - Builds strength, focus, and stability.
   - Embodies the archetype of the Warrior, fostering courage and resilience.
2. **Mountain Pose (Tadasana)**
   - Promotes grounding and a sense of inner power.
   - Encourages presence and alignment with purpose.
3. **Plank Pose (Phalakasana)**
   - Strengthens the core, symbolizing inner stability and strength.
4. **Tree Pose (Vrksasana)**
   - Enhances balance and connection to the earth.
   - Encourages a calm and centered masculine presence.

Yoga sequences can be tailored to specific intentions, whether to release tension, cultivate strength, or foster relaxation.

Meditation for Masculine Empowerment

Meditation is a practice of mindfulness and stillness that connects the mind and body. For queer men, it offers a way to cultivate clarity, focus, and emotional resilience while anchoring masculinity in the present moment.

Meditation Practices for Masculinity

1. **Grounding Meditation**
   - Visualize roots growing from your feet into the earth, anchoring your body in stability and strength.
   - Use affirmations such as "I am grounded, powerful, and present."
2. **Breath Awareness Meditation**
   - Focus on the breath as it moves in and out of your body.
   - Imagine each inhale filling you with strength and each exhale releasing tension.
3. **Masculine Archetype Visualization**
   - Picture yourself embodying the King, Warrior, Magician, or Lover archetype.
   - Reflect on the qualities you wish to cultivate and how they feel in your body.
4. **Body Scan Meditation**
   - Bring awareness to each part of your body, releasing tension and inviting a sense of wholeness.

Regular meditation fosters a sense of inner calm and empowerment, providing a foundation for navigating life's challenges.

Somatic Experiences for Healing and Empowerment

Somatic practices focus on the body as a site of healing and transformation. They involve intentional movements and sensations that release trauma, build self-awareness, and foster emotional regulation.

Somatic Practices for Queer Men

1. **Ecstatic Dance**
   - Move freely to music, allowing the body to express emotions and release stored tension.
   - Focus on how each movement feels, rather than how it looks.
2. **Grounding Exercises**
   - Stand barefoot on the ground and feel the connection to the earth.
   - Use slow, deliberate movements to center yourself in the present moment.
3. **Breathwork Sessions**
   - Engage in guided breathwork practices to release emotional blockages and awaken inner energy.
   - Techniques such as diaphragmatic breathing or the Wim Hof Method can be particularly empowering.

4. **Touch Therapy**
   - Explore safe and consensual forms of touch, such as massage or self-soothing gestures, to reconnect with your body and foster self-acceptance.

Somatic practices help bridge the gap between mind and body, creating a holistic sense of masculinity that is deeply felt and authentically expressed.

Integrating Physical Practices into Daily Life

Embodied masculinity is not achieved through occasional effort but through consistent practice. Incorporating yoga, meditation, and somatic experiences into your daily routine helps anchor empowerment in both ordinary and extraordinary moments.

Suggestions for Integration:

1. **Morning Rituals**
   - Begin the day with a short yoga sequence or grounding meditation to set the tone for strength and presence.
2. **Movement Breaks**
   - Take time during the day for intentional movement, such as stretching, dancing, or breathwork, to release tension and re-center.

3. **Evening Reflection**
    - Conclude the day with a body scan meditation or a gentle somatic practice to process emotions and foster relaxation.
4. **Community Practices**
    - Join yoga classes, meditation groups, or dance gatherings that celebrate diversity and inclusion, building connection and support.

The Power of Embodied Masculinity

Embodied masculinity is a dynamic, lived experience that integrates strength, vulnerability, and authenticity. For queer men, it offers a way to reclaim the body as a source of power and wisdom, moving beyond societal constraints and toward a fuller expression of self.

Through yoga, meditation, and somatic experiences, we anchor empowerment in the body, transforming abstract ideas of masculinity into tangible, felt realities. These practices not only foster personal growth but also create ripples of connection and healing in our communities.

Will you step into the practice of embodied masculinity and anchor your power in the present moment? The body is your foundation, and the journey begins here.

Part 5: The Queer Male as Healer and Visionary

The Queer Prophet: Redefining Leadership

Throughout history, gay men have been visionaries, healers, and cultural disruptors, often occupying roles that bridge the physical and spiritual realms. As outsiders to many traditional structures, queer men possess a unique perspective that allows us to see beyond the limits of societal norms and imagine new possibilities. This ability makes us natural prophets—leaders who guide cultural and spiritual evolution by challenging outdated paradigms and inspiring transformation.

The queer prophet redefines leadership not as dominance or authority but as a service to humanity's collective growth. By embodying authenticity, compassion, and creativity, we create pathways for others to follow, empowering communities to embrace diversity and align with a higher vision of connection and inclusivity.

The Role of the Queer Prophet

A prophet is not merely a foreteller of the future but a visionary who illuminates the path toward progress. For queer men, this role involves:

- **Catalyzing Change**: Questioning and dismantling systems of oppression and exclusion.
- **Embodying Authenticity**: Living as an example of truth and self-acceptance, inspiring others to do the same.
- **Bridging Worlds**: Integrating masculine and feminine energies, spiritual and material realms, and individual and collective needs.
- **Nurturing Growth**: Guiding others toward greater understanding, empathy, and empowerment.

The queer prophet draws upon personal experiences of marginalization and resilience to advocate for a world where all voices are heard, and all identities are celebrated.

Redefining Leadership

Traditional models of leadership often emphasize control, hierarchy, and conformity. The queer prophet rejects these outdated notions in favor of a leadership style that is inclusive, collaborative, and visionary.

Principles of Queer Leadership:

1. **Empathy and Connection**: Prioritizing relationships and understanding others' needs and perspectives.
2. **Creativity and Innovation**: Approaching challenges with imagination and a willingness to think outside the box.
3. **Courage and Authenticity**: Leading by example, even when it involves taking risks or facing resistance.
4. **Service and Collaboration**: Viewing leadership as an opportunity to uplift others and foster collective success.

By embracing these principles, queer men redefine leadership as a force for healing and transformation, rather than domination or exclusion.

The Healer and Visionary Within

Queer men have historically been seen as spiritual guides and healers in many cultures, such as the two-spirit individuals of Indigenous communities or the shamanic roles of gender-fluid figures in ancient societies. These traditions recognize our ability to embody duality, balance, and insight, making us uniquely equipped to guide others through change and growth.

Healing Through Visionary Leadership:

1. **Restoring Wholeness**: Helping individuals and communities integrate the parts of themselves that have been fragmented or suppressed.
2. **Challenging Norms**: Questioning societal structures that perpetuate harm and inequality.
3. **Creating Safe Spaces**: Building environments where authenticity and vulnerability are celebrated.
4. **Inspiring Hope**: Offering a vision of a better future, grounded in inclusivity, compassion, and shared purpose.

As healers and visionaries, queer men play a vital role in fostering collective evolution, helping humanity move toward greater balance and harmony.

Queer Men as Catalysts for Cultural Evolution

The queer prophet's leadership extends beyond individual transformation to address broader cultural shifts. Our unique perspectives challenge traditional norms and inspire innovation in art, politics, spirituality, and more.

Areas of Cultural Impact:

1. **Art and Expression**: Using creativity to explore and celebrate diverse identities and experiences.

2. **Activism and Advocacy**: Championing causes that promote equality, justice, and human rights.
3. **Spirituality and Healing**: Reimagining spiritual practices to include and affirm marginalized voices.
4. **Community Building**: Creating networks of support and solidarity that uplift and empower.

By embracing our roles as cultural catalysts, queer men help shape a world where individuality is honored, and collective well-being is prioritized.

The Spiritual Evolution of Leadership

Queer prophets not only challenge societal structures but also inspire spiritual evolution. This involves fostering a deeper connection to the divine and encouraging others to see themselves as integral parts of the greater whole.

Spiritual Practices for Visionary Leadership:

1. **Meditation and Reflection**: Developing clarity and insight through regular spiritual practice.
2. **Sacred Storytelling**: Sharing personal experiences and truths to inspire and educate others.
3. **Rituals of Transformation**: Creating ceremonies that mark milestones and foster community growth.
4. **Aligning with Archetypes**: Drawing upon the wisdom of the King, Warrior, Magician, and Lover to guide leadership.

Spiritual leadership is not about imposing beliefs but about fostering a sense of interconnectedness and shared purpose.

The Challenges of Queer Leadership

Being a queer prophet often involves navigating resistance, misunderstanding, or even hostility. These challenges can be daunting, but they also provide opportunities for growth and resilience.

Overcoming Challenges:

1. **Cultivate Inner Strength**: Build a foundation of self-awareness and self-acceptance to weather external opposition.
2. **Find Allies**: Surround yourself with supportive individuals and communities who share your vision.
3. **Focus on the Bigger Picture**: Remember that leadership is not about immediate results but about creating lasting change.
4. **Embrace Vulnerability**: Recognize that challenges are part of the journey and a source of strength and wisdom.

By facing these challenges with courage and grace, queer men model resilience and inspire others to do the same.

The Call to Visionary Leadership

The world is in need of leaders who can bridge divides, inspire transformation, and guide humanity toward a more inclusive and compassionate future. As queer men, we are uniquely equipped to answer this call, drawing upon our experiences, insights, and innate ability to navigate duality.

The queer prophet is not merely a figure of the past but a role we are called to embody today. Through authenticity, creativity, and a commitment to service, we can redefine leadership and shape a world that honors the full spectrum of human experience.

Will you embrace your role as a queer prophet, healer, and visionary? The path may be challenging, but it is also one of profound purpose and possibility. Step forward, and let your light guide the way.

Sacred Sexuality: Healing Through Pleasure

Honoring the Sacredness of Queer Intimacy and Relationships

Sacred sexuality is the recognition that intimacy, pleasure, and connection are profound spiritual experiences. For queer men, this perspective transforms our relationships and desires into pathways for healing, empowerment, and transcendence. In a world that often stigmatizes queer intimacy, reclaiming the sacredness of our connections is an act of defiance, self-love, and spiritual growth.

By embracing sacred sexuality, we honor the divine within ourselves and our partners. It becomes not only an expression of love and pleasure but also a practice of healing and self-discovery. Through this lens, sexuality is no longer merely physical—it is a communion of body, mind, and spirit.

Understanding Sacred Sexuality

Sacred sexuality is about approaching intimacy with intention, presence, and reverence. It invites us to see our sexual energy as a powerful force for creation and transformation. This energy is not limited to physical acts; it encompasses emotional vulnerability, spiritual connection, and the exchange of energies between individuals.

For queer men, sacred sexuality is especially meaningful because it allows us to reclaim our desires and identities from societal shame or judgment. It affirms that our love, bodies, and connections are inherently sacred, deserving of celebration and respect.

The Healing Power of Pleasure

Pleasure is often dismissed or undervalued in discussions of healing, yet it is one of the most potent tools for transformation.

Sacred sexuality reframes pleasure as a pathway to self-awareness, self-acceptance, and connection.

Ways Pleasure Heals:

1. **Releases Shame**: By embracing pleasure, we confront and dissolve societal stigmas that have been internalized.
2. **Builds Connection**: Shared pleasure fosters intimacy and trust, deepening bonds with partners.
3. **Reduces Stress and Trauma**: Physical and emotional pleasure activates the body's natural healing mechanisms, such as the release of endorphins and oxytocin.
4. **Celebrates the Body**: Pleasure reminds us that our bodies are sources of joy and vitality, not just vessels of appearance or function.

When approached mindfully, pleasure becomes a sacred act of healing and empowerment.

Queer Intimacy as Sacred

Queer intimacy often exists outside traditional structures, offering opportunities to redefine relationships in ways that align with our values and truths. Sacred sexuality invites us to honor these connections as spiritual experiences, rooted in authenticity and mutual respect.

Practices to Honor Queer Intimacy:

1. **Create Ritual Space**: Transform your intimate encounters into sacred rituals by setting an intentional space with candles, music, or meaningful objects.
2. **Eye Gazing**: Begin by looking deeply into your partner's eyes, connecting on a soul level before engaging physically.
3. **Mindful Touch**: Focus on the sensations of touch, being fully present with your partner's body and energy.
4. **Speak Intentions**: Share your desires, boundaries, and affirmations, creating a foundation of trust and understanding.

By treating intimacy as a sacred exchange, we deepen its impact and create a safe space for vulnerability and connection.

Healing Through Relationships

Sacred sexuality also extends to the way we approach relationships. Whether romantic, platonic, or sexual, these connections are opportunities for healing and growth.

Key Principles of Healing Relationships:

1. **Mutual Respect**: Honor each other's boundaries, desires, and individuality.
2. **Open Communication**: Create a spacc for honest conversations about needs, fears, and feelings.
3. **Shared Vulnerability**: Allow yourself to be seen fully, encouraging your partner to do the same.

4. **Intentional Growth**: Use the relationship as a mirror, reflecting areas where healing or transformation is needed.

Relationships are not just about companionship or pleasure; they are sacred partnerships that support mutual evolution.

Exploring Sacred Sexuality Through Practices

There are many ways to incorporate sacred sexuality into your life, enhancing both personal and shared experiences.

Solo Practices:

1. **Self-Compassion Rituals**: Treat your body with kindness and care, exploring touch and movement as acts of self-love.
2. **Meditative Breathwork**: Combine breath with visualization, imagining energy flowing through your body and expanding your sense of pleasure.
3. **Affirmations of Worth**: Speak words of affirmation that honor your body, desires, and identity as sacred.

Partnered Practices:

1. **Tantric Breathing**: Sync your breath with your partner's, creating a flow of energy and connection.
2. **Energy Exchange**: Use touch, intention, and presence to feel the energetic exchange between you and your partner.

3. **Gratitude Sharing**: After intimacy, express gratitude for your partner and the experience, reinforcing the sacred bond.

These practices foster deeper connections and transform intimacy into a spiritual act.

Releasing Shame and Embracing Joy

Many queer men carry shame around their desires or identities due to societal conditioning. Sacred sexuality provides a framework for releasing this shame and embracing the joy of who we are.

Steps to Release Shame:

1. **Acknowledge the Shame**: Recognize where it comes from and how it affects your relationship with intimacy.
2. **Reframe Desires as Sacred**: Affirm that your desires are natural, valid, and a source of divine connection.
3. **Seek Safe Spaces**: Surround yourself with people and communities that affirm and celebrate your identity.
4. **Celebrate Pleasure**: Actively engage in experiences that bring joy and connection, reinforcing the sacredness of your sexuality.

Releasing shame is not a one-time act but an ongoing process of self-acceptance and healing.

The Gift of Sacred Sexuality

Sacred sexuality is a gift—a way to honor the divine within and to connect with others on a profound level. For queer men, it is a powerful tool for reclaiming our identities, healing past wounds, and celebrating the unique beauty of our connections.

By approaching intimacy with intention and reverence, we transform it into an act of empowerment, healing, and transcendence. Sacred sexuality affirms that our bodies, desires, and relationships are not only valid but sacred, deserving of celebration and respect.

Will you embrace the sacredness of your sexuality and relationships? The journey begins with the simple yet profound act of honoring yourself and those you love. Step into the sacred, and discover the transformative power of healing through pleasure.

Creative Masculinity: Art, Play, and Self-Expression

How Creativity Becomes a Transformative Masculine Power

Masculinity, in its fullest expression, is dynamic, multifaceted, and generative. Creativity is one of its most transformative powers, offering a way to express individuality, process emotions, and shape the world with intention and vision. For queer men, creativity is not just a tool for self-expression—it is a lifeline that nurtures authenticity, heals wounds, and builds bridges to understanding and empowerment.

Creative masculinity transcends traditional notions of manhood, which often confine men to rigid roles of strength, control, or practicality. Instead, it celebrates the power of imagination, play, and artistic expression, allowing men to redefine masculinity as an expansive and evolving force.

The Essence of Creative Masculinity

Creative masculinity is the ability to channel masculine energy into acts of creation and expression. It is the impulse to build, inspire, and explore, balanced by the vulnerability required to share one's inner world. This creativity is not limited to traditional art forms but includes all expressions of originality and individuality, from storytelling to innovation to problem-solving.

For queer men, creative masculinity serves as a counterbalance to the societal pressures of conformity. It invites us to embrace our unique perspectives, using creativity as a way to honor and celebrate our identities.

Art as a Path to Empowerment

Art is one of the most powerful ways to access and express creative masculinity. Whether through painting, writing, music, or performance, art allows us to tell our stories, explore our emotions, and share our truths.

How Art Empowers Masculinity:

1. **Exploring Identity**: Art provides a space to delve into and articulate aspects of identity that may feel complex or unspoken.
2. **Processing Emotions**: Through creative expression, we can navigate pain, joy, and everything in between, transforming emotions into something tangible and meaningful.
3. **Creating Visibility**: Sharing art helps queer men assert their presence in a world that often overlooks or marginalizes us.
4. **Inspiring Others**: Art has the power to connect, educate, and uplift, fostering empathy and solidarity.

Art is not about perfection; it is about authenticity. It is a means of shaping the world by sharing a piece of yourself with it.

The Power of Play

Play is often overlooked as a masculine strength, yet it is one of the most essential aspects of creativity. Play sparks joy, encourages exploration, and nurtures a sense of curiosity. For queer men, play is a way to reclaim the freedom to express ourselves without fear of judgment.

How Play Fuels Creativity:

1. **Encourages Risk-Taking**: Play invites us to try new things without fear of failure, fostering innovation and resilience.
2. **Breaks Down Barriers**: Through humor, movement, or games, play dissolves rigid expectations and fosters connection.
3. **Stimulates Imagination**: Play allows us to think beyond the practical or possible, opening doors to new ideas and solutions.
4. **Releases Stress**: Play reminds us that life is not solely about productivity; it is also about joy and presence.

Incorporating play into daily life, whether through physical movement, games, or spontaneous creativity, strengthens our ability to adapt and thrive.

Self-Expression as Liberation

Self-expression is a cornerstone of creative masculinity, offering a way to break free from societal constraints and embrace individuality. For queer men, self-expression often involves reclaiming parts of ourselves that have been silenced or hidden.

Forms of Self-Expression:

1. **Personal Style**: Clothing, accessories, and grooming can be powerful forms of self-expression, reflecting identity and creativity.

2. **Storytelling**: Sharing personal narratives through writing, speaking, or performance fosters connection and visibility.
3. **Movement**: Dance, yoga, or other forms of embodied expression allow us to communicate through the physical self.
4. **Advocacy**: Using creativity to amplify causes and messages we care about merges self-expression with purpose.

Self-expression is an act of courage and freedom, transforming the personal into the universal.

The Healing Power of Creative Masculinity

Creativity is inherently healing. It allows us to confront and process pain, reconnect with our inner selves, and imagine new possibilities. For queer men, creative masculinity is a tool for reclaiming our stories, releasing shame, and finding joy in self-discovery.

Healing Through Creativity:

1. **Reframing Pain**: Turning struggles into art reframes them as sources of strength and wisdom.
2. **Building Confidence**: Sharing creative work fosters self-esteem and a sense of accomplishment.
3. **Connecting with Others**: Creative expression creates opportunities for shared understanding and mutual support.

4. **Celebrating Individuality**: Embracing creativity affirms that our uniqueness is a source of beauty and power.

When we engage with creativity, we tap into the transformative potential of masculine energy, channeling it toward growth and healing.

Practices to Cultivate Creative Masculinity

Daily Practices:

- **Free Writing or Journaling**: Set aside time to write without judgment, exploring thoughts, feelings, or ideas.
- **Doodling or Sketching**: Use art as a way to relax and process emotions, without worrying about the final product.
- **Dance or Movement**: Incorporate physical movement that feels expressive and freeing.
- **Playful Exploration**: Experiment with new hobbies, interests, or activities to awaken curiosity.

Community Practices:

- **Join Creative Groups**: Participate in art, writing, or performance workshops that celebrate diversity and inclusion.
- **Collaborate**: Create with others, merging perspectives and strengths.
- **Share Your Work**: Whether through social media, open mics, or community events, share your creativity with the world.

By prioritizing creativity, we honor the masculine power of creation and connection.

Creative Masculinity as Transformation

Creative masculinity is not merely about producing art or engaging in play—it is about embodying the ability to shape and transform the world. It reminds us that masculinity is not confined to tradition or rigidity but is a dynamic and generative force.

For queer men, creativity becomes a way to redefine masculinity, celebrate individuality, and heal the wounds of marginalization. It empowers us to imagine and create a world that reflects our truths and honors our diversity.

Will you embrace the power of creative masculinity to transform your life and the world around you? The canvas is blank, and the possibilities are endless. Let your creativity lead the way.

Queer Brotherhood: Building Authentic Connections

Fostering Community and Support Within the LGBTQ+ Space

Queer brotherhood is a profound bond that transcends shared identities and experiences, offering a sense of belonging, connection, and solidarity. For queer men, authentic connections within the LGBTQ+ space are essential for fostering community, healing past wounds, and creating a foundation of mutual support. In a world that often marginalizes or isolates us, queer brotherhood serves as a sanctuary where we can be seen, valued, and uplifted.

Building queer brotherhood is an act of empowerment, inviting us to embrace our shared humanity while celebrating the diversity of our community. It is about creating spaces where vulnerability is met with compassion, where differences are honored, and where collective strength becomes a source of individual growth.

The Importance of Queer Brotherhood

Queer men often grow up without traditional models of brotherhood that affirm their identity. Societal norms can isolate us, creating a sense of disconnection from others and even from ourselves. Queer brotherhood addresses this by offering a space where:

- **Belonging**: We feel understood and accepted without the need to hide or conform.
- **Healing**: Past wounds caused by rejection, bullying, or discrimination can be addressed through supportive relationships.
- **Empowerment**: Collective strength inspires confidence and the courage to live authentically.
- **Celebration**: Shared experiences and achievements are honored, creating a sense of joy and pride.

Queer brotherhood is a vital antidote to isolation, fostering community that nurtures and sustains us.

Fostering Authentic Connections

Authentic connection is the heart of queer brotherhood. It requires vulnerability, mutual respect, and a commitment to understanding one another. For queer men, this often involves unlearning societal norms that encourage competition, hierarchy, or emotional detachment.

Steps to Build Authentic Connections:

1. **Create Safe Spaces**: Establish environments where individuals feel free to express themselves without fear of judgment.
2. **Practice Active Listening**: Show genuine interest in others' experiences, affirming their feelings and perspectives.
3. **Share Your Story**: Vulnerability invites connection; sharing your journey encourages others to do the same.
4. **Offer Support**: Be present for others in moments of need, showing empathy and compassion.
5. **Celebrate Diversity**: Recognize that each person's identity and experience adds richness to the community.

Authentic connections thrive when they are built on trust, openness, and mutual care.

Building Community in LGBTQ+ Spaces

LGBTQ+ spaces are vital hubs for queer brotherhood, providing opportunities to connect, collaborate, and grow. Whether physical or virtual, these spaces serve as platforms for building relationships and fostering a sense of belonging.

Types of LGBTQ+ Spaces:

1. **Social Groups**: Meetups, clubs, and gatherings where queer men can form friendships and share experiences.
2. **Support Networks**: Groups focused on mental health, recovery, or navigating specific challenges within the community.
3. **Creative Communities**: Spaces for art, performance, or activism that celebrate queer voices and talents.
4. **Online Platforms**: Digital communities that provide connection across geographic boundaries.

By engaging in these spaces, queer men create networks of support that extend beyond individual relationships, strengthening the community as a whole.

The Challenges of Queer Brotherhood

While queer brotherhood offers profound opportunities for connection, it is not without its challenges. Internalized biases, unresolved trauma, and societal pressures can sometimes create barriers to building authentic relationships.

Common Challenges and How to Overcome Them:

1. **Competition and Comparison**: Shift focus from competition to collaboration, recognizing that each person's journey is unique and valuable.
2. **Fear of Vulnerability**: Practice small acts of openness, gradually building trust with others.
3. **Cliques and Exclusion**: Advocate for inclusivity within groups, ensuring that all voices are welcomed and respected.
4. **Navigating Differences**: Approach conflicts or misunderstandings with empathy and a willingness to learn.

Queer brotherhood thrives when we address these challenges with honesty and compassion, fostering a culture of mutual respect and support.

Celebrating the Diversity of Queer Brotherhood

The LGBTQ+ community is beautifully diverse, encompassing a wide range of identities, experiences, and perspectives. Queer brotherhood celebrates this diversity, recognizing that our differences enrich and strengthen us.

Ways to Celebrate Diversity:

1. **Intersectionality**: Honor the unique experiences of queer men who navigate multiple identities, such as race, ethnicity, or ability.

2. **Generational Connections**: Build bridges between younger and older queer men, sharing wisdom and experiences.
3. **Global Solidarity**: Engage with queer communities from different cultures, learning from their stories and struggles.
4. **Allyship Within the LGBTQ+ Spectrum**: Support and celebrate individuals across the spectrum, fostering unity and collaboration.

By embracing diversity, queer brotherhood becomes a powerful force for inclusion and growth.

Practices to Strengthen Queer Brotherhood

Building queer brotherhood requires intentional effort, but the rewards are immeasurable. The following practices can help foster stronger bonds and a more connected community:

1. **Host Gatherings**: Organize events that bring queer men together for conversation, celebration, or collaboration.
2. **Mentorship**: Offer guidance and support to younger queer men, sharing lessons and experiences.
3. **Collaborative Projects**: Work on creative, social, or advocacy projects that unite individuals around a shared purpose.
4. **Rituals of Connection**: Create ceremonies or traditions that honor milestones, relationships, or community achievements.

These practices create opportunities for meaningful connection, ensuring that queer brotherhood remains vibrant and dynamic.

The Power of Queer Brotherhood

Queer brotherhood is more than friendship—it is a profound bond that affirms our worth, nurtures our growth, and celebrates our shared humanity. For queer men, it is a lifeline in a world that often marginalizes or misunderstands us, offering connection, healing, and empowerment.

By fostering authentic connections and building inclusive communities, we create a foundation of support that extends beyond individual relationships. Queer brotherhood becomes a source of collective strength, inspiring us to live authentically and work toward a more inclusive and compassionate world.

Will you step into the circle of queer brotherhood and help build a community that celebrates and uplifts us all? The bond is waiting to be forged, and its potential is limitless.

Part 6: Embodying the Divine Masculine

The Divine Masculine in Action

Daily Practices to Live as an Integrated and Empowered Individual

The Divine Masculine is not just a concept quer archetype; it is a way of being that informs how we live, connect, and contribute to the world. For queer men, embodying the Divine Masculine means integrating its qualities—strength, purpose, compassion, and authenticity—into everyday life. It involves aligning thoughts, emotions, and actions with the highest expression of masculinity, creating a life of empowerment and integrity.

Through intentional daily practices, we bring the Divine Masculine into action, transforming abstract ideals into tangible experiences that shape our relationships, work, and personal growth. These practices serve as anchors, grounding us in authenticity and guiding us to live with purpose and presence.

The Qualities of the Divine Masculine

To embody the Divine Masculine, we must first understand its qualities. These traits reflect a balanced and empowered approach to life:

1. **Strength**: Resilience and the ability to stand firm in one's truth while supporting others.
2. **Purpose**: A clear sense of direction and alignment with one's values.
3. **Compassion**: Empathy and care for others, balanced with self-respect.
4. **Authenticity**: Living true to oneself, free from fear or pretense.
5. **Creativity**: The power to build, innovate, and transform.
6. **Presence**: The ability to remain grounded and engaged in the moment.

These qualities are not static; they evolve as we grow and integrate new experiences. The key is to embody them with intention, using daily practices to cultivate and express them.

Daily Practices to Embody the Divine Masculine

Morning Rituals: Setting the Tone for the Day

1. **Grounding Meditation**: Begin each day with a short meditation to center yourself. Visualize roots growing from your feet into the earth, connecting you to stability and strength.
2. **Affirmations**: Speak or write affirmations that align with the Divine Masculine, such as "I am grounded in my purpose" or "I act with strength and compassion."
3. **Physical Movement**: Engage in exercises like yoga, stretching, or strength training to awaken your body and embody resilience.
4. **Journaling**: Reflect on your intentions for the day, focusing on how you want to embody the Divine Masculine in your actions and interactions.

Throughout the Day: Practicing Presence and Integrity

1. **Mindful Actions**: Approach each task with focus and intention, whether at work, in relationships, or during personal time.
2. **Compassionate Communication**: Listen actively and speak with kindness, balancing honesty with empathy.

3. **Boundary Setting**: Practice saying yes to what aligns with your purpose and no to what does not, protecting your energy and time.
4. **Acts of Service**: Find small ways to uplift others, whether through encouragement, assistance, or simply being present.

These practices help integrate the Divine Masculine into your daily life, fostering alignment between your values and actions.

Evening Rituals: Reflecting and Renewing

1. **Gratitude Practice**: Reflect on the day and identify moments where you embodied the Divine Masculine. Give thanks for the lessons and growth they brought.
2. **Body Scan Meditation**: Tune into your body, releasing tension and connecting with its wisdom.
3. **Creative Expression**: Spend time on a creative activity, such as journaling, drawing, or music, to channel the energy of transformation and innovation.
4. **Set Intentions for Tomorrow**: Reflect on how you can deepen your embodiment of the Divine Masculine in the coming day.

Evening rituals create space for self-reflection and renewal, ensuring that each day builds upon the last.

Integrating the Divine Masculine in Relationships

The Divine Masculine thrives in connection with others. In relationships, it manifests as support, authenticity, and balance.

Practices for Relational Empowerment:

1. **Active Listening**: Be fully present during conversations, validating the other person's experiences and emotions.
2. **Shared Purpose**: Collaborate with partners, friends, or community members on goals that align with your values.
3. **Vulnerability**: Share your thoughts and feelings openly, creating spaces for mutual growth and understanding.
4. **Leadership with Compassion**: Guide and inspire others with empathy and respect, fostering collective empowerment.

By embodying the Divine Masculine in relationships, we cultivate deeper bonds and contribute to a culture of mutual support and respect.

Overcoming Challenges in Embodying the Divine Masculine

Living as an integrated and empowered individual is not without its challenges. Old patterns, societal expectations, or personal insecurities may create resistance.

Strategies for Overcoming Challenges:

1. **Self-Awareness**: Regularly check in with yourself to identify areas of growth or misalignment.
2. **Seek Support**: Connect with mentors, peers, or communities that affirm and encourage your journey.
3. **Practice Forgiveness**: Be compassionate with yourself when you fall short, using setbacks as opportunities to learn and grow.
4. **Stay Grounded in Purpose**: Revisit your values and intentions often, using them as a compass to navigate difficulties.

Challenges are part of the process, offering opportunities to deepen your understanding and embodiment of the Divine Masculine.

The Ripple Effect of Embodied Masculinity

When we live as integrated and empowered individuals, the impact extends beyond ourselves. Embodied masculinity inspires others, strengthens communities, and contributes to a culture of authenticity and growth.

Ways Embodied Masculinity Impacts the World:

1. **Leadership by Example**: Living with integrity inspires others to do the same.
2. **Healing Relationships**: Embodied masculinity fosters connection, understanding, and mutual respect.

3. **Community Empowerment**: By aligning with purpose and authenticity, we contribute to collective growth and transformation.
4. **Cultural Evolution**: Redefining masculinity creates space for diverse and inclusive expressions of identity.

The Divine Masculine in action is not just about personal fulfillment—it is a force for positive change in the world.

The Journey of Embodiment

Embodying the Divine Masculine is not a destination but a lifelong journey. It requires consistent practice, reflection, and a willingness to grow. Each day offers new opportunities to align with this energy, to integrate its qualities, and to live as a source of strength, compassion, and purpose.

Will you take the next step in embodying the Divine Masculine? The path is yours to walk, and the transformation it brings is as profound as it is empowering. Begin today, and let the Divine Masculine guide your journey toward wholeness and impact.

Epilogue: The Future of Masculine Consciousness

Envisioning a World Healed and Uplifted Through the Queer Divine Masculine

The journey of embodying the queer divine masculine is not just about personal growth or individual empowerment—it is about creating a ripple effect that transforms the world. When queer men step into their roles as healers, visionaries, and leaders, they bring balance to a culture that has long been dominated by distorted expressions of masculinity. In doing so, they redefine what it means to be masculine and lay the groundwork for a future of inclusivity, compassion, and shared purpose.

The future of masculine consciousness is not bound by the limitations of the past. It is expansive, fluid, and alive, honoring the interplay of strength and vulnerability, individuality and community, action and reflection. In this vision, the divine masculine becomes a healing force, bridging divides and fostering harmony in a world that desperately needs it.

The Evolution of Masculine Consciousness

Masculine consciousness has undergone profound shifts throughout history, moving from archetypes of dominance and control to emerging models of collaboration and balance. The queer divine masculine represents the next evolution—a blend of tradition and innovation that embraces duality and diversity.

In this future:

- **Strength** becomes the courage to lead with compassion and integrity.
- **Power** is redefined as the ability to uplift and empower others.
- **Connection** is prioritized over competition, creating a foundation of mutual respect and support.

- **Creativity** is celebrated as a means of transformation and innovation.
- **Spirituality** is interwoven with daily life, grounding masculine energy in purpose and presence.

This evolution is not a rejection of masculinity but a reclamation of its highest potential, offering a blueprint for living with authenticity and impact.

The Role of the Queer Divine Masculine in Healing

Queer men, as natural bridge-builders and boundary-breakers, are uniquely positioned to lead this evolution. Our experiences of navigating duality, challenging norms, and embracing authenticity give us the tools to model a new way of being.

How the Queer Divine Masculine Heals the World:

1. **Challenging Toxic Masculinity**: By embodying strength without aggression and power without domination, we offer an alternative to harmful masculine ideals.
2. **Fostering Inclusivity**: Our ability to celebrate diversity inspires others to do the same, creating communities that value all identities and experiences.
3. **Promoting Emotional Resilience**: Through vulnerability and openness, we normalize the expression of emotions as a source of strength.
4. **Creating Sacred Spaces**: We design environments where healing, connection, and growth are prioritized, benefiting individuals and the collective.

Queer men, as stewards of the divine masculine, contribute to a world where everyone is empowered to live authentically and harmoniously.

A World Healed Through Masculine Consciousness

Imagine a world where the divine masculine is fully embodied—where men of all identities are free to live as their most authentic selves, guided by purpose, compassion, and creativity. In this world:

- **Families and Communities** thrive on mutual respect and shared leadership.
- **Systems and Institutions** are restructured to prioritize inclusivity, fairness, and well-being.
- **Art and Innovation** flourish, fueled by the creative energies of diverse voices.
- **Conflict and Division** are addressed with wisdom and empathy, fostering healing and reconciliation.

This vision is not a utopia but a possibility—a future we co-create by embracing the principles of the queer divine masculine and living them in our daily lives.

The Call to Action

The future of masculine consciousness begins with each of us. Every choice we make, every relationship we nurture, and every action we take contributes to the collective evolution. By embodying the divine masculine, we become catalysts for change, modeling a new way of being that inspires and uplifts those around us.

Steps to Contribute to the Future of Masculine Consciousness:

1. **Live Authentically**: Embrace your truth and share it with courage and pride.
2. **Cultivate Community**: Build connections that celebrate diversity and foster mutual support.
3. **Lead with Compassion**: Use your power to uplift others and create spaces of healing and growth.
4. **Model Integration**: Show the world that strength and vulnerability, action and reflection, can coexist in harmony.

The call to embody the divine masculine is not just an invitation—it is a responsibility. By answering this call, we contribute to a future that honors the sacred in all its forms.

A Closing Vision

The queer divine masculine is a gift to the world, offering a pathway to healing, empowerment, and unity. It teaches us that masculinity is not a fixed ideal but a living, evolving energy that thrives on balance and connection.

As we step into this vision, we reclaim masculinity as a force for good—one that uplifts, inspires, and transforms. In this

future, the divine masculine becomes a beacon of hope and possibility, guiding humanity toward a more inclusive and compassionate world.

The journey is ongoing, and the destination is one we create together. Will you walk this path and embody the future of masculine consciousness? The world is waiting for your light, your strength, and your vision. Step forward, and let the divine masculine shine through you.

Notes